CONTEMPORARY ISSUES IN POLITICAL THEORY

Contemporary Issues in Political Theory

Robert Booth Fowler
Associate Professor of Political Science
University of Wisconsin—Madison

Jeffrey R. Orenstein
Associate Professor of Political Science
Kent State University—Stark

JOHN WILEY & SONS

New York • Santa Barbara • London • Sydney • Toronto

Library of Congress Cataloging in Publication Data:

Fowler, Robert Booth, 1940-
    Contemporary issues in political theory.

    Includes indexes.
    1. Political science.   I.   Orenstein, Jeffrey R.,
joint author.   II.   Title.
JA66.F65   320.5   76-7410
ISBN 0-471-27031-8
ISBN 0-471-27032-6 pbk.

Printed in the United States of America

10 9 8 7 6 5 4 3 2 1

Preface

Many college textbooks contain a dedication "To My Students." This one does not because we have written it *for* you instead of *to* you. We have tried to convey some of the excitement and satisfaction we find in the exploration of normative political theory. All too often, political theory is introduced in an abstract manner that anesthetizes intellectual curiosity and deadens living issues. We have avoided this through a clear contemporary analysis of the terms, topics, and issues to illuminate political theory and stimulate thinking and investigation of further problems and applications of it. We have tried to help the process along by assuming no advanced knowledge, by writing with as much clarity as possible, by being well organized, and by providing a general introduction, suggestions for further reading, and a useful index.

We have presented normative theory with enough eclecticism to fit into the organization of a variety of courses in political science. In particular, this book could be the core of a topically organized course and equally as effective as a supplement to an historical or analytical course in political theory. Although it is written for the student of political science, its utility clearly extends to introductory history or philosophy students as well—indeed, to anyone who can benefit from a discussion of the moral dimension of public events and institutions.

This book covers the major topics of political theory that occupy a basic position in any scheme of political values. We have chosen these topics for their seminal significance and have looked at them in depth in order to introduce their complexities, to suggest some of their historical roots, and to evaluate their relationships to other issues as well as their contemporary significance. Thus, our topics embrace anarchy, democracy, justice, liberty and equality, and obligation and revolt.

v

This book is a product of the postbehavioral revolution, written by authors who have experienced modern political science training as well as the insights of political theory, and is designed for students who may know or want to know empirical political analysis as well as Platonic political analysis. We have not rejected the valid findings of modern social scientific approaches nor have we slighted insightful contributions of ancient or modern political theorists. We have combined both perspectives in this book.

The text is also well suited to be the core of the section on normative political theory that is part of many courses that are general introductions to political science. Since it does not have any antiempirical bias, it does not dismiss all political science as a mere footnote to Aristotle, a view that has prevented many present and former works from appealing to those with more eclectic interests in the discipline.

The introduction covers basic terminology, methodological issues, sources of political thought, and relates political theory to other humanistic approaches to public life. The discussion of issues commences with a question often talked about by citizens but hardly ever looked at by political scientists: Do we need politics and government at all and, if so, what kind(s) makes moral as well as practical sense? The classic confrontation between anarchists and statists is resolved in an unconventional case for politics and government that accepts many of the insights of philosophical anarchists and yet gives government a clear but morally limited justification. Throughout the book we are conscious of the growing skepticism about political life today, and we recognize that the question of the value of politics cannot be taken blithely for granted in this age of cynicism and technological terror, if indeed, it ever should have been.

Our treatment of democracy carefully explicates several competing democratic theories, particularly pluralism, populism, and participatory democracy. The arguments for and against each are evaluated and accompanied with a guide for the student to understand the conceptual and empirical assumptions that often underlie each.

Our analysis of liberty and equality follows next, since both are so closely related to familiar ideas of democracy. We define several of the contending versions of liberty and equality and discuss their historical origins. The analysis includes an argument for particular ways of understanding liberty and equality that is morally justifiable and conceptually plausible. Considerable effort is spent demonstrating the mutual relations between liberty and certain aspects of equality.

Recognizing the increasing importance of discussions of justice, we explore the topic and its alternative visions in detail. We assess the relative merits and weaknesses of leading theories, including John Rawls'. We also suggest a framework for a theory of justice that might be congruent with defensible conceptualizations of democracy, liberty, and equality demanded by modern political life.

One of the most burning issues of modern political thought—political obligation—is covered in a similar manner: when are people obligated, or not obligated, to the polity? This ancient question remains one of the most fascinating and vexing of issues in our discipline. We consider the most significant answers to the dilemmas posed by political obligation and the morality surrounding it while formulating an answer of our own.

The conclusion focuses on perhaps the most discussed and least understood issues of political theory: revolt and revolution. When may citizens overthrow their government? When are their obligations changed or canceled? We consider these questions in the context of the rest of normative political thought, in view of the related questions of democracy, justice, liberty, equality, and obligation, among other things. As you might expect, an adequate analysis of the subject ranges from Socrates to Camus, from passive disobedience to active revolution.

We are confident that this odyssey through the sometimes exciting, sometimes frustrating, issues and insights of political theory will be a useful guide for you and will serve to heighten your moral sensitivity to the myriad dimensions of public life. The need for moral perspective, combined with accurate factual knowledge about politics and government, has never been greater than in this age of global politics. We hope that this book is instrumental in leading you toward such a perspective.

Robert Booth Fowler

Jeffrey R. Orenstein

Contents

CONTEMPORARY ISSUES IN POLITICAL THEORY

Introduction

Political theory concerns the search for moral truth in politics. It considers what *ought* to exist in political life. This book discusses several significant issues, including justice, liberty, democracy and obligation, which are central to contemporary political theory.

This chapter provides a brief, but hopefully vital, introduction to political theory itself. It is scarcely possible to study—much less practice—political theory without defining what political theory does and does not encompass. We also require an understanding of (1) how political theory is normally practiced and (2) what standards we use in order to distinguish good political theory from the bad. Finally, we must have some idea of how people may and do justify political values.

ON THE NATURE OF POLITICAL THEORY

Political theory is a special form of discourse, a conversation between thoughtful people who seek to learn and communicate about what is right in a moral sense in politics. Like all forms of theory, political theory involves the search for truth, but this does not necessarily mean an odyssey toward immutable laws or universal norms. For some thinkers it may do so, but for others the truths will be less certain, less broad, and far more tentative. Perhaps political theory can provide many in our skeptical age with no more than limited insights or intimations into partial truths and clouded suns. But the search for truth is the essential task of political theory. This quest is also, in our view, necessarily ethical. The truth we seek is how humans *should* behave and judge in political life. The quest is, inescapably, for moral guidance.

Sometimes political theory as we understand it is termed "normative" since it is directed toward discovering norms by which we should live. Yet we do not devote our efforts exclusively to explicating normative positions on the subject of liberty and justice and the like. While we do make normative arguments, there are other important problems that concern us as students of political theory.

Political theory involves not only the formulation of a moral position in politics, but also a logical or analytic consideration of political concepts. This reflection on basic concepts, such as equality and obligation, is vital because they are the foundation blocks for every political theory. To construct an argument in political theory about the nature and significance of justice, we must reflect on the alternative meanings of justice, what it suggests, what it implies. We do this in the case of every key concept we use in the following chapters. We discuss concepts like liberty and equality in everyday language—what they seem to mean to us—as well as how they have been comprehended and explained by other political thinkers past and present.

In addition to our discussion of basic concepts, we also analyze several alternative resolutions to the problems we treat. We do this to acquaint the student with some of the main views on such subjects as the proper stance regarding justice or obligation and because political theory necessarily involves this kind of analysis. Only by knowing and arguing about alternative perspectives can we strengthen our own argument and communicate with others who hold differing viewpoints. Only by analysis can we assure ourselves that we have considered opposing views, taken them seriously, and honestly endeavored to garner whatever fruits they may offer. When we discuss political obligation, for instance, we eventually argue normatively in political philosophy, trying to defend a certain manner of understanding obligation and its implications in the political sphere. But we do so only after a careful analytical investigation of a number of possible alternatives.

No matter how thoroughly we pursue the three main aspects of political theory—reflection on basic concepts, analysis of alternative views and the pursuit of normative truth—we must remember that political theory is unique as a philosophical subject because it is conducted in a specifically political context. There is no easy definition of politics; it is too complicated an enterprise. Yet most Westerners would agree that politics encompasses conflicts and agreements in the public realm. It is this public aspect that is the crucial defining feature, one that distinguishes politics (however imperfectly) from those parts of life that we all consider more immediately private, personal, and limited. Thus political theory certainly must include questions of justice, because justice concerns the proper relations among people in such obviously public arenas as the law or the distribution of economic goods. It must include political obligation because this is a relationship among citizens. But it rarely includes the relations between a brother and a sister or between lovers or between a man and his flower garden and evening pipe.

WHAT POLITICAL THEORY IS NOT

We do not pretend that our conception of political theory is the only possible one, but it is not unusual. It is, however, a view that excludes certain types of activity, and we should clarify what we do not count as political theory, since this would help make apparent what we do mean by our enterprise. In particular, political theory does not mean six types of activity that are sometimes confused with it: ordinary opinion, ideology, practical politics, policy judgments, history, and political science.[1]

Political theory is not ordinary opinion because political theory, unlike opinion, can be sustained by reasoned analysis and justification. To have an opinion on justice or liberty is not to have a thoughtful argument developed by consideration of the concept of justice, analysis of the alternative visions of justice, and careful argument for the truth of one vision. Opinion is usually casual and lacking matured reflection and justification. In this sense we do not believe that most people are ordinarily political philosophers, even though they may have opinions about justice, equality, and many other matters in politics.

On the other hand, we do not think political theory should be equated with the development or advocacy of an ideology, a world view that is all encompassing, held to be absolutely true and action oriented. Political theory involves no propounding of total visions nor any rush to mandated action. Instead, it involves reflection, intellectual search, argument, and painstaking enlightenment. It is not a place to rest, a surrender of the mind to a faith, but an invitation to thought, to communication, to argument. It is not the realm of dogmatists, but of thinkers.

We do not contend that political theory is unrelated to action, nor do we deny that for many people its most important function is to obtain guidance for their performance as citizens. But we do not think that this is its only function. Nor is it true that any one of us can expect whatever political principles we are able to

---

[1] Donald W. Hanson, "The Nature of Political Philosophy" in D. Hanson and R. B. Fowler, *Obligation and Dissent* (Boston: Little Brown, 1971).

develop can be easily translated into specific recommendations for particular circumstances or immediate policy choices. The purpose of political theory is to examine the nature of broader concepts such as liberty and democracy rather than give policy makers instant advice as to proper decisions. A thorough grounding in the principles of political theory surely can illuminate many policy choices and particular normative dilemmas in politics, but it cannot do more. There is a considerable distance between the general and the specific, a reality that sometimes annoys those who want political theory to provide quick policy advice. This reaction is understandable, but so is the reaction of many political theorists who complain that the people who are entirely policy oriented do not look to the broader normative context and the wider realm of principle—without which their policy decisions lack needed perspective.

Political theory should also be distinguished from history, although so often it is not. We respect the history of political thinking, but we do not think it is a substitute for the ongoing process of new thinking. It is for just this reason that we have chosen to follow an approach in this book that concentrates on political theory as a living normative and analytical process rather than a study of great thinkers of the past. The historical approach, the process of reducing political theory from an active enterprise to a review of what others in the past have taught, often if not always, diverts us from molding our own political theory. It often transforms us into passive observers of the work and times of Hobbes or Marx, but does not enable us to craft any political theory for ourselves.

Moreover, an exclusively retrospective focus often ignores the fact that all our exemplars in this activity need not be historical. Political theory, often of a high order, occurs today as well as yesterday (and presumably always will). The discipline goes on. John Rawls' *A Theory of Justice* or Robert Nozick's *Anarchy, the State & Utopia* are two recent and outstanding examples.

Of course, we realize that the past constitutes a vast repository of great political theory, one that we draw on freely and gratefully in our essays in this book. We also acknowledge, as every student must, that the way we think about contemporary problems has been set largely by others who have gone before, and we often give due recognition to those great thinkers. But we are determined to see those who earlier visualized liberty, for instance, in ways that we cannot ignore, as partners with the present in an enduring search for the nature and worth of liberty.

The great tradition of Western thought, the inevitable background of contemporary political theory, may be viewed in several ways, all valuable for us. This tradition, spanning the centuries from the Greeks of ancient Athens to great nineteenth-century thinkers such as Mill, Marx, and Freud, forms a body of thought that is valuable on its own. Its investigation can be, and for us often is, a voyage into the history of particular eras and places, a way to expand and sensitize our minds, as well as an aesthetic pleasure. But we see it in the context of this book as primarily a resource. This resource constitutes a debate between men and women as concerned in the past as we are in the present with enduring (if not always identical) problems of political morality—from justice to political obligation to liberty. We dare not ignore this vast historical treasury in studying contemporary political theory, any more than we should make the exploration of its riches a substitute for our own efforts in political theory.

Finally, political theory is not identical (although it may at times be congruent) with most of what we think of today as political science. There is no universal agreement on the points of difference, but two are usually noted. The first concerns the contrasting goals of most modern political theorists and political scientists. We know political theorists are mainly concerned to discover truth about how men and women *should* live together in political communities. The fundamental focus is *ethical* and not necessarily factual. It concentrates on what is morally *right* rather than on facts or theories about how people actually behave at this time. At its heart is the task of value judgment. Political science, however, ordinarily seeks to discover how men and women act in political life, seeking to formulate, if possible, laws that may govern political behavior. In political science, man is viewed as an object no different in principle from the objects of physics or chemistry, and the study of his behavior seeks to be as free of value judgments as possible, although few political scientists think that this is an easy or completely possible goal.

Second, political science differs from political theory in method. Political science employs a basically inductive method. That is, political scientists try to test their theories about political behavior by inducing factual evidence of their accuracy from the empirical world around us. The crucial test of the truth of their assertions about the real world is their correspondence with the world of fact or, in alternative conceptions, their nonfalsifiability by facts derived from the empirical world. Political theory, in contrast, rarely employs inductive evidence in making arguments for one position or another. Its characteristic approach is not to *prove* one position or another, but to make rational arguments—sometimes using linguistic, utilitarian, or, most often, deductive arguments—deducing its truths from first principles found in nature, the human person, or history.

It is the first difference that is probably the crucial one. Political science is usually a contrasting activity to political theory because political science, like all science, searches for the truths that describe how things actually occur, while political theory focuses on how we ought to behave. Neither activity is somehow superior to the other. Both are demanding tasks and both are worthwhile, yet they should not be confused. It is one thing to describe how Congress operates or to formulate a theory about how democratic legislatures in general function and test it with facts drawn from the actual practice of contemporary democratic legislatures and another to argue how democratic legislatures should operate or whether we should have democratic government at all.

Political science and political theory often overlap each other. For example, most, if not all, political theories do contain empirical claims or assertions, since arguments about what ought to be in politics will involve some considerations of the world of fact. One of the great weaknesses of many political theories, now as in the past, is that they do not conscientiously attempt to justify their empirical component according to the canons of scientific activity. Political writings abound in statements, for example, about human nature or behavior and about the operation of political systems and the like, with scant factual basis for them beyond the illusions of personal intuition or "common sense." This is never acceptable.

POLITICAL THEORY, GOOD AND BAD

There are no inflexible guidelines that denote what good political theory is, but there are some well-understood principles that most practitioners have always invoked to characterize good political theory. We think five are particularly significant and worthy of mention in order to assist you in assessing our arguments to follow and your own efforts.

First, we must know, as clearly as possible, what the basic values (or the fundamental premises) are that underlie any argument in political theory, whether on justice or liberty or the like. Time and again arguments are undermined by vague or ambiguous basic premises. This failure to make clear the underlying norm(s) can easily be a fatal mistake. Making them clear means more than merely identifying the position from which you start. It also means endeavoring to defend it, turning it over and thinking aloud or on paper about it until it emerges as a richly explored starting point.

Second, we need to recognize that many arguments in political theory fail because their first premises and values lack justification. All too often no justification is offered for the basic value(s) on which an argument is built. So important and so often so neglected is this aspect that we explore some of the ways people can, and sometimes do, justify political viewpoints.

Third, good political theory requires that basic rules of deduction, logic, and consistency be followed. Very often normative arguments in politics are grounded in a series of deductions from first premises, which do not really follow logically. A classic example was the argument that liberal democracy is the appropriate form of government once we realize that there are no ultimate truths for politics.[2] The argument went like this: assuming there are no absolute answers, it is logical to deduce that tolerance is a vital value, since we would not

[2]Thomas L. Thorson, *The Logic of Democracy* (New York: Holt, Rinehart and Winston, 1962).

want to close off any choices, and then, agreeing that tolerance is what we want to encourage, it follows that liberal democracy is the most appropriate political system as it is most committed to tolerance—hence the so-called "logic of democracy." But a little consideration shows that this is an egregious example of poor deduction and dubious logic. First, there is no *necessary* logic to the claim that because there are no answers, therefore we should support tolerance: we might or we might not. Second, even if we endorsed tolerance, it would not necessarily follow that liberal democracy (majority rule and minority rights) would give us the most tolerance; this would be a matter for empirical investigation.

Consistency is important too, consistency in continuing to base an argument on the same fundamental value(s) and not assuming one at the beginning of an argument and quite another at the end, consistency as well in using key words and concepts in the same way throughout an entire argument. For example, it is hard to take seriously an argument about liberty that alters the meaning of liberty six or seven times during its course. Nothing seems more obvious and yet it is not always easy to avoid this common and dangerous fallacy.

Fourth, in addition to the importance of being clear about basic values and their justification and carefully seeking to be consistent and logical, a satisfactory political theory must demonstrate a good deal of breadth. It must cast a wide net of argumentation, incorporating many sides and views of a problem into its own treatment. In treating justice, for instance, it should show awareness of how justice is talked about in the present time and how it has been considered in classic formulations of the past. It must not ignore crucial dilemmas and pitfalls without which no sophistication can be developed. Indeed, it should properly confront its own formulations with others. Far too often, practitioners of political theory do not ask themselves what objections others would hold of their view. This not only diminishes the appeal that any argument can make to others, who may well have differing perspectives, but it also deprives political theorists of the strengthening that can result from a rigorous challenge to their viewpoint. Positions and values are not self-evident; they have to be defended; and, fortunately, in defending them they either get better or they fall. Without challenge they are untested and vulnerable.

Finally, good political theory must provide insight into the problem it tackles. Great political theorists like Plato and Hobbes are admired political theorists because what they had to say about politics and human life provides precious insight even now. What is unique about many of the greatest thinkers in the long tradition of political thought is that they were able to look at familiar problems (such as liberty, obligation, or justice) and see them in rather original ways, casting a new light that is creative and educational. This is the most basic requirement of all—and the most challenging.

JUSTIFICATIONS FOR POLITICAL VALUES

Most of us tend to assume that our values are self-evident, that our positions are obvious, and that many of the objections to them are ridiculous. At the same time, when we are pressed to defend our political values or to impose them on others, many of us tend to take a relativist stance. We say that our values are fine for us and that other people's values are fine for them. Popular as these two approaches are, and often as they are found in the same person, neither approach fulfills one of the crucial standards for a good political theory: the need for a clear and thoughtful justification of our basic norms.

Sooner or later every political argument will work its way back to ultimate values and justifications for them, and there is no way this task can be escaped or wished away. Arguments about a version of democratic politics, for instance, eventually lead back to what grounds we justify it on. Consequently, one of the most important and demanding requisites for any political theory is an awareness of ultimate principles of justification and the reasons for them.

We all know that this is as difficult a problem as we can find in political theory. Time and again we have all had arguments that seemed to come to a dead end because the two sides were traced back to fundamentally opposing root values justified on alternative grounds that did not seem reconciliable. It is not our purpose in this book to resolve these basic conflicts, since we devote our attention to specific political values and not how they are ultimately justified. But it is essential to begin a book on political theory with a clear-headed recognition that justifications do differ, to understand what some of the fundamental positions are, and to appreciate that having a well-understood basis of final justification is mandatory for every political theory, no matter how broad its sweep and no matter how specific its focus.

There are four general types of justification that political theorists have employed, and several have important subdivisions that are equally as significant. None is more popular today in the United States among thoughtful people, perhaps, than the position of ethical relativism. Ethical relativists believe that the only legitimate justification for values in politics is personal preference and they deny that there are any absolute truths in politics. These proponents, like supporters of other perspectives, insist that people should frankly admit the basis of their norms—in this case, their subjective judgments or feelings—and avoid pretending that there may be fancier or more impressive bases. As they see it, there are two prime advantages to the relativist justification. The first teaches us that no one has any business being too quick or too confident in proclaiming what others ought to believe or ought to do—for, after all, everybody has their own ideas. Who can say with certainty that others' ideas are wrong? Second, they maintain that once people learn to get along quite well with the reality of ethical relativism it provides a basis for each individual's values, which is all we need as long as people practice some tolerance toward others.

One form of ethical relativism is the emotive theory of ethics, developed by A. J. Ayer in *Language, Truth and Logic*.[3] According to this analysis, ethics, including political theory, has its roots in our feelings, and can only be understood in this context. Of course, many psychoanalysts and political psychologists, beginning with Freud, have agreed. According to some of these thinkers, when we take a stance in political theory we are expressing our feelings and possibly also urging others to accept our feelings. Hence the label that some have applied to this form of ethical relativism: the ethics of "boo-hurrah." For some analysts this fact is a sad one, since it seems to imply that reason does not play much of a role in political theory; but others are not so pessimistic, contending that we can reason a good deal over political norms as long as we remember that in the end we have no final justification except our feelings. They believe the real danger comes from people who do not understand themselves well enough to realize that their values are grounded in subjectivist sentiments and tend to talk of absolute truths. For they suspect that people can too easily move from talk to action, imposing their subjective wills on others in the name of grand absolutes that, in the end, are no more than individuals' personal feelings.

Another version of ethical relativism talks less about feelings and concentrates more on experiences. According to this outlook, propounded, for example, by the British thinker Michael Oakeshott,[4] our political values express our particular experiences in life, the habits we form, and the customs we learn. They can be expressed in rational terms, and they should be, but all rational justifications are more or less rationalizations for our individual experiences. This analysis also urges the wisdom of open justification by the canons of ethical relativism, for there is no other conceivable source for values. There are no absolute truths, only particular experiences and the consequent necessity for tolerance if we are going to live together.

A second form of justification is the existentialist position. Existentialists view the relation between individuals and their world as absurd, not only without absolute meaning but also without any meaning. They believe it is preposterous to think that any political values can be justified in absolute terms. What the individual is left with is the stark reality of a life often filled with pain and only guaranteed to end in death. We have, so to say, our existence, but no truths, no essences, to guide us. Existentialists advocate that what everyone must do in these circumstances is *choose* values, including political norms, to follow in life. They urge that we choose as thoughtfully and as rationally as possible, but choose with a clear-headed understanding that we can never be certain of the

---

[3]A.J. Ayer, *Language, Truth and Logic* (New York: Dover, 1952).
[4]Michael Oakeshott, *Rationalism in Politics* (New York: Basic Books, 1962).

correct answer. The problem they see is that many choose, in Jean Paul Sartre's phrase, in "bad faith." They choose political norms that they hope will allow them to choose no more and avoid the responsibility that choice entails, that will allow them to escape the inescapable reality that there is no absolute answer and no avoidance of responsibility. People cling to political ideologies, religious systems, and totalitarian hopes, rather than courageously keeping their options open and going on day after day choosing as situations arise. The existentialist test, then, for an adequate justification of a political norm is whether it is self-consciously and thoughtfully *chosen* and whether it continues to keep the individual aware of the necessity of ongoing *choices*—and the *responsibility* for them.

A third group of justifications that are often employed in political philosophy follows quite another direction. It is the group that maintains that political values must have, and can have, absolute justifications. One form is the eternally attractive and popular natural law argument that holds that one or more political values are absolutely true for all times, places, and people. Sometimes natural law arguments take the form of asserting that there are certain duties or laws that are incumbent on all of us. This was the position of the classic natural lawyer St. Thomas Aquinas. He contended that God set down certain norms that were permanently binding and that must always be obeyed to the best of fallible human ability. Another form is rather more familiar to Americans—the natural rights argument. This viewpoint declares that there are certain rights, such as life or liberty, which are guaranteed by nature (or God through nature) to all people forever. It becomes the duty of governments to protect and to realize these rights. The classic expression of this position is in our own Declaration of Independence. A third variety that is widespread among a number of contemporary thinkers claims that there are certain basic needs that all humans have because they are human beings, and they insist that it is a matter of absolute right that they ought to be fulfilled.

Whatever the form, most natural law justifications, since they are absolute and universal in character, tend to be a source of frustration for those who do not share such justification for their particular values. There is no doubt that there is a long distance between those who are ethical relativists and those who believe in natural rights. Yet such differences of justification do not necessarily require that political philosophies need to differ in substance. An advocate of natural rights and an ethical relativist may agree or, at least, communicate on many values, from the centrality of liberty to the importance of property.

Other forms of justification that are absolute in their character include those that draw on history. There is the Marxist justification, that the dialectical processes of history provide the essential justification for what is right in politics. Consider Marx's views on the capitalist order as an example. Marx is often erroneously interpreted as believing that capitalism was an unmitigated evil, while in fact Marx believed that when history brought capitalism to a nation, it was a good thing. On the other hand, when historical processes brought capitalism toward its demise, as they inevitably would, then capitalism was no longer a good system, no longer annointed by history. Another version of the historical justification, which is also influential today, is the conservative argument from tradition. Many conservatives explicitly or implicitly make past history, or a certain version of it, into an absolute value that manifests the culmination of human wisdom and that ought not to be transgressed.

A final set of justifications are those that try, sometimes awkwardly, to steer between the relativist and the absolutist positions. These include pragmatism, utilitarianism, and dependence on the wisdom of experts. Pragmatists maintain that the test of political values ought to be their concrete worth in practice, their workability in speaking to situational human needs. Though this approach is common in the United States, it is a weak justification in its more ordinary form. For to justify something on its practicality involves the assumption that X is practical for achieving Z without telling us why it is that we want to get to Z. That is, it does not really provide us with any genuine basis for our ultimate values, for our Zs.

Much more satisfactory is the utilitarian justification. This justification suggests that values are good if they promote the greatest good for the greatest number or if they advance the public interest. While the public interest is a notoriously vague concept, and it is not too easy to measure what the greatest good for the greatest number might be, most versions of the utilitarian test aspire to find a justification that is neither a buttress for absolute values nor merely a matter of individual whim, but one that allows judgments in light of a desire to benefit the public at large. This justification, of course, involves an assumption about what is useful, and consequently it often incorporates what Stephen Toulmin thinks is the necessity of proceeding with the assumption that one is giving "good reasons" based on the shared value framework of a given cultural framework. This is a limitation, but Toulmin, among others, assert that this is a reality we must accept.[5]

Another variety, proposed by T. D. Weldon in his classic *The Vocabulary of Politics*,[6] suggests that we think about justification in political theory the way art critics think about art. His idea is that art and political theory share a common dilemma in that neither can have recourse to any absolute standards. Yet he notes that this does not prevent the world of art from reaching considerable agreement on which paintings are great because there are well-known and widely shared norms for good art that are upheld and developed by those who are most experienced in the study of art—the art critics. He proposes that

[5]Stephen Toulmin, *Reason in Ethics* (Cambridge, England: Cambridge University Press, 1968).
[6]T. D. Weldon, *The Vocabulary of Politics* (Baltimore: Penquin Books, 1953).

political critics—those who know the most about political theories as well as politics itself—ought to be seen as the source of what constitutes good political theory. They ought to be the best form of justification for the adequacy of a political theory or a political system.

No matter how many justifications there are, and no matter which one we may rely on, the most important preliminary requirement for a decent political theory is that there be one, and that it be laid clearly on the table so that all may see from where it is that we start. It is much harder to argue about ultimate justifications than it is about substantive positions regarding justice or political obligation, and disputes about justification are not as central to political theory as are such questions as liberty or justice. But an adequate political theory must have a clearly posited justification.

SUGGESTIONS FOR SUPPLEMENTARY READING

Barry, Brian *Political Argument* (New York: Humanities Press, 1965).

Germino, Dante, *Beyond Ideology: The Revival of Political Theory* (New York: Harper & Row, 1967).

Hanson, Donald W., "The Nature of Political Philosophy" in D. Hanson and R. B. Fowler, *Obligation and Dissent* (Boston: Little Brown, 1971).

Murphy, Joseph S., *Political Theory: A Conceptual Analysis* (Homewood, Ill.: Dorsey Press, 1968).

Oppenheim, Felix, *Moral Principles in Political Philosophy* (New York: Random House, 1968).

Quinton, Anthony, *Political Philosophy* (New York: Oxford University Press, 1967).

Tinder, Glenn, *Political Thinking: The Perennial Questions,* (Boston: Little Brown and Co., 1974).

Toulmin, Stephen, *Reason in Ethics* (Cambridge, England: Cambridge University Press, 1968).

Sabine, George, *A History of Political Theory,* (New York: Holt, Rinehart and Winston, 1961).

Sibley, Mulford Q., *Political Ideas and Ideologies* (New York: Harper & Row, 1970).

Spitz, David, Ed., *Political Theory and Social Change* (New York: Atherton, 1967).

Weldon, T. D., *The Vocabulary of Politics* (Baltimore: Penquin Books, 1953).

Wolfe, Alan and Charles McCoy, *Political Analysis: An Unorthodox Approach* (New York: Crowell, 1972).

Politics, Government, and Democracy

I

Political theory directs us to many fascinating and important issues in the ethics of political life. Contemporary political theory must deal with many substantive issues, from political obligation to justice to revolution, but none are more important nor more intriguing than the subjects of this chapter. The very utility of the omnipresent state and the best form of it are at the heart of today's political dialogues no less than they have been for ages. No subject is more controversial than the value of organized politics and yet none is more of a foundation for the other central questions in political theory. If politics is not a worthy activity then surely democracy, obligation, and justice are not worth analysis since they are concepts that revolve around politics and the political order.

That the value of politics is under attack is familiar to contemporary Americans after a decade or more of divisive foreign policy and a scandal in leadership morality, but the problem is not a uniquely American one. Revolutions, revolts, and demonstrations around the world indicate the seemingly universal mood of dissatisfaction with governments and politics as usual. The fallout from Watergate, scandals in Europe, and the failure of public officials to fulfill the lofty promises in nations that recently threw off the yoke of colonialism stimulates widespread disgust with politicians and politics, a finding substantiated by our neighbors as well as political polls, low voter turnouts, and support for rebels in various parts of the world.

There is nothing inevitable about these sentiments, since British public opinion, for example, has a much higher regard for its political figures and processes in spite of Britain's weighty political problems. There is evidence that Americans, in particular, have held politics in low esteem for a long time. We should note, however, that throughout history there have always been people, from Aristotle to Jefferson to Camus, who have affirmed the validity and utility of political communities, denying that politics was necessarily unsavory, corrupt, or boring. The debate between those thinkers who doubt the worth of politics and those who either view it as a necessary if limited good or who place great hope in political activity, dreaming of it as one of the most glorious of human endeavors, is one of the most significant public questions humanity must face.

A second basic question that logically flows out of the first, is whether we ought to have a specifically political community at all, especially as embodied in an organized government. Politics may have its uses, may even be a natural attribute of people, but do we need to have a state? This may appear to be a strange question, for all societies we know have governments and we are well socialized to think of anarchists as crazy advocates of chaos. But it is not self-evident that the path of morality leads to the justification of the existence of governments. The question needs to be investigated in detail. All of us have at least a trace of the anarchist in our souls in the resentment we harbor toward the state at tax time or when we are thwarted by laws we think are stupid or when we consider the vast sums of money squandered by military machines. Certainly the history of political thought contains many anarchists whose utter contempt for the immorality of governments in theory and practice has led them to press for the destruction of the state, although not necessarily of politics. Their claims deserve careful analysis.

We suggest that politics and even organized governments have a great deal of utility, although the anarchists have made many telling points that cannot be ignored. This truth becomes apparent when we consider the interrelated question of the nature of the best kind of state, of who should rule and by what authority. The present, like past history, abounds in an almost infinite variety of ideals of government and sets of rulers, each loudly proclaiming its legitimate authority. Dictators, oligarchies of the rich, military juntas, Marxists, and other more or less democratic systems all proclaim themselves to be the embodiment of legitimacy. We conclude that only governments that are firmly democratic in practice as well as rhetoric, those resting on popular participation and responsiveness, may validly make this claim. It should be made clear from the outset, however, that there is no need to commit ourselves to the orthodox Western idea of representative democracy. Democracy is considerably broader than the American or British experience.

This leads to a fourth and final concern of this chapter: What is the most legitimate form of democracy? Our age, as any other, still hears the charge that the major existing "democratic" states are merely hollow images of "true" democracy. Using both the insights of the anarchists and the statists, we ask what democracy really is and what form of it is best. These are basic questions because they cut to the heart of the justification and character of the states that we all live with. They are so basic that they must be analyzed before we can move to more complex values like justice, liberty, equality, obligation, or revolt, which are based on viewpoints of appropriate perspectives on these foundation questions.

II

POLITICS

What is politics? Is it a valuable human activity? Can it be dispensed with? Should it be? After all, it is not perfectly obvious that politics is particularly important and it is certain that many citizens from the most ordinary people of today to the great religious prophets of yesterday have not thought it was. But political science students, public officials, and many political philosophers take it for granted that politics deserves our interest and our participation. How do we decide who is right?

There is no single or simple definition of politics, but, as our discussion of the meaning of politics in Chapter 1 makes evident, we see politics concerned with the *public* integration of human needs and possibilities. It involves conflict and concensus in the public realm over who gets what, when, how, and why in society. It is about what roads are built, what TV stations are licensed, who supplies our electricity at what cost, and what politicians are elected, if any. It is also about other things than the scramble for tax dollars, welfare, subsidies, and elections. It involves such moral questions as the appropriateness of pornography, TV violence or gun control, spiritual and religious matters such as the relation between church and state, and symbolic questions such as the treatment of the flag or the observance of patriotic holidays.

Since there are many opinions about the relative value of politics, there are many sides to this eternal debate. Four views in particular merit our attention: the idea that politics is of limited use for society as a whole, that it is of use for personal needs, that it is the highest human enterprise, or that it lacks any kind of genuine value.

Politics as Limitedly Useful

The viewpoint that politics has uses for society as a whole, but only if its range of concerns and demands is carefully delimited, is the ordinary perspective of most Americans by all indications. They reflect a long popular viewpoint, first articulated in an undeveloped manner by the Greek philosopher Epicurus in the fourth century B.C.[1] Many agree with Epicurus that politics is a permanent feature of human affairs, since people inevitably form groups and seek to gain their own—and, hopefully, general—benefit from public activity. Some modern proponents insist politics is especially necessary today, because we must live together in large, complex, and expanding social orders that contain great possibilities of social conflict. They feel that politics may assist us as we try to live together with a minimum of conflict and a maximum of cooperative and fair dealing, and, consequently, they contend it is wise to accept politics in order to get what limited help we can from it.

Advocates of the limited use theory of political activity repeatedly stipulate that politics can never be more than a tool for societies and individuals. Just as it is foolish to pretend that we can do without politics, so is it dangerous to make politics an end in itself. Many people feel that the sinful or selfish nature of people is more determinate of human behavior than political activity could ever be and, thus, that politics can not be that significant an enterprise. Reinhold Niebuhr, a great American religious and political thinker of the twentieth century, developed this perspective. Niebuhr argued that too much involvement and faith in politics can easily lead to political fanaticism, concentration camps, and the murder of millions. Those who become too devoted to political life can lose perspective and make serious mistakes; the greatest danger is that they may overestimate what politics (and government) can accomplish in this world of sin, habit, custom, and popular political apathy. They may try to force people to adhere to a particular vision of the good society at great popular sacrifice. Niebuhr also argues, along with many others who wish to acknowledge the value of politics while stressing its limits, that politics should not be confused with features of life that are not means but ends that constitute what is truly worthwhile in human experience. Politics should not be confused with life itself, with God, with love and joy, nor with family and friends. Against them politics is secondary.[2]

Politics as Fulfilling Personal Needs

Another image of politics, distinct from the first and yet related to it as another position of moderately skeptical acceptance of politics, sees political life as an

---

[1] Epicurus in W. J. Oates, Editor, *The Stoic and Epicurean Philosophers* (New York: Modern Library, 1940).
[2] R. Niebuhr, *The Children of Light and the Children of Darkness* (New York: Scribners, 1944).

activity that is justifiable if it fulfills one's *personal* needs for fun, excitement, or power. Sometimes, as Harold Lasswell argued a generation ago, it may even be the vehicle for displacement of dangerous neurotic private needs and compulsions from the dark side of our souls.[3] In one way or another, however, this is the political disposition that dominates many actual and would be officeholders and politicians. It is an attitude that grips endless student interns in state legislatures and administrative offices in Washington, D.C. It is the driving energy for many of the young and old who participate in political campaigns by licking envelopes, canvassing, or giving advice and money. Not all interns are there for these reasons, nor does this set of motivations activate all party workers and politicians, but anyone who has worked in any of these capacities knows how many of those involved in politics have little vision of its public value as compared with their keen appreciation of its personal value to them.

This approach to politics is, perhaps, harmless enough as long as its practitioners do not have much power or influence. But when it is the view of politics held by people with great power, then serious questions must be raised. The objective of politics becomes the self-satisfaction of those who participate in it, rather than more vital public ends. Winning may then become all important, as may supporting a winner, for there is far more power and excitement in being on top of politics (or anything else) than being on the bottom. Perspective and vision of general public purpose slip away.

There is the danger that the politician, or the student politico can become narrow in his or her excessive preoccupation with one dimension of life. It is also partly that he or she can lose sight of any principles besides success and political loyalty. The truth is that this obsessive slant on politics led straight to the abuses uncovered in the Watergate scandals, where powerful people lost concern for anything but the necessity of maintaining their personal power through political victory.

Politics as the Highest Human Enterprise

Third, there are those whose view of the political dimensions of life involves a commitment that goes far beyond what many people give to politics or respect in others who choose to do so. They argue that politics is far more important and far nobler than views that limit its reach or make it a matter for the mere satisfaction of personal needs. This perspective ranks politics as the highest human enterprise because it claims that we must focus on how people live together and the best way to do it successfully. We cannot avoid problems concerning how we shall live together and thus we cannot avoid politics. In fact, we ought to dedicate ourselves to it rather than hoping it will go away. No task, the enthusiasts say, could possibly be more vital to us. Consequently, no task could be

[3]H. Lasswell, *The Political Writings* (New York: Free Press, 1951).

more honorable because our humanity is the most honorable thing we possess.

The ancient Greeks of classical Athens celebrated the tremendous worth of politics, which is why they honored great politicians and statesmen over all other men. They felt politics was the highest human activity. Many supporters of participatory democracy today also praise politics. For them direct popular self-government through political activity is the essence of the good life (see Chapter 3). The ideal of service for the public among British aristocrats over the past several centuries illustrates the same inclination. The same applies to some of America's political "aristocrats" such as the Kennedys, the Rockefellers, and the Roosevelts. No one can deny their interest in the power and excitement of politics, but it would be perverse to ignore their considerable devotion to the principle of public service, often at great personal cost to health, family, and fortune.

In the period since World War II a number of eloquent political thinkers have defended this perspective. Some, like Hannah Arendt, contend that politics is so unsatisfactory today because it has forgotten the belief of the ancient Greeks that political action is the best mechanism humans have for personal and political growth. Others, like the late Albert Camus, stress their belief that only in active political communities can men and women achieve the personal dignity and social development that is the highest human ideal. All agree that our distaste for politics in its best and most responsible forms amounts to an unnecessary surrender of our own human potentialities and a retreat to human privatism and selfishness that is as personally self-defeating as it is socially disastrous.[4]

The problem that this perspective confronts in the West in our time is that few really believe it. We do not perceive that politics is more important than family life or, often, religion. Clearly it plays a much smaller role in the existence of the average person than does work or family. In addition, many persons have reason to observe that the ideal of public service or even active political agitation about such issues as racial equality requires a good amount of time or money. It also necessitates a good deal of energy that few have after a long day's work in societies that make economic work so important and public service so remote. Few except an elite of upper middle class or wealthy people can readily devote themselves to politics. We must remember that Athens was a slave society.

Another kind of objection to this approach makes quite a different point. Many contemporary social scientists, most famously Bernard Berelson, warn against the uncritical celebration of the ideal of active involvement in politics. They say that widespread participation or commitment in politics is dangerous. Berelson and others perfer a largely inactive or apathetic populace. They fear that mass mobilization or intense interest in politics activates a large number of citizens who are ignorant about political issues and candidates and who bring

---

[4]H. Arendt, *On Revolution* (New York: Viking Press, 1963).
A. Camus, *The Rebel* (New York: Vintage Press, 1956).

only irrationality to the political process. Others have noted that intense mass participation can lead swiftly to totalitarian tyrants and demagogues. They cite the intense political atmosphere of the early 1930s when Hitler came to power as a case in point.[5]

These theorists claim that investing politics with great importance tends to raise absurdly inflated expectations about what it can do in alleviating human ills or in achieving human happiness. The result will be inevitable, and sometimes dangerous, disappointments when politics turns out to be unable to usher in Nirvana or Utopia. They have a point, but it is never simple to decide when the politics of promise and activism goes too far in its faith and raises too many hopes. Some conservatives, for example, have accused Lyndon Johnson of causing substantial psychic hurt to millions of America's poor by declaring a War on Poverty in the middle 1960s that included extravagant claims about abolishing poverty in one generation. They ask, what good was there in promising what politics could not—and did not—produce?

Yet it must also be pointed out that politics in some form always goes on. The apathetic may be "safe" when they remain quiescent, but we must surely realize that by their acquiescence, by our apathy, we always grant those who do believe in politics control over our lives. The apathetic are never masters of their political destiny, and they are all too often the victims in human history. Those who celebrate apathy may often be political conservatives wearing the clothes of neutral social scientists.

Nor should we forget, amid warning about the dangers of too much politics, the uses of some politics. For politics and political action have produced changes. They produced constitutions, civil liberties, and even (for better or for worse) the modern welfare state. Politics' value must not be ignored even as its dangers are acknowledged.

Politics is Irrelevant

Juxtaposed to these viewpoints, a final and enduring popular conception of politics not only denies that politics is the highest human enterprise but also argues that it is not of much use at all. This is a common view of politics in the United States, although it seems perplexing to political science students and professors, not to mention politicians.

One aspect of this perspective contends that there is no way anybody can make politics relevant to truly crucial aspects of human existence, such as family, work, faith, or the rhythm of ongoing nature. For the average person, job, family, or friends occupy the central places in their lives. Even watching a baseball game at home on TV, watering the lawn, perparing for a daughter's wedding, or going bowling with friends attract far more people in a day than

[5]B. Berelson et al., *Voting* (Chicago: The University of Chicago Press, 1954), pp. 311–323.

dozens of political rallies in a year because these many other features in life appear to be more vital to their daily existence.

Another aspect emphasizes the paramount significance of religion over all else, very much including political activity. Such disparate religious teachers as Tolstoy, Lao Tzu, and many Christian mystics teach that only religious salvation matters. Sainthood or "The Way" beckon us and we must not tarry with such transient, worldly, and evil concerns as politics. Others, such as some nineteenth-century anarchists or the famous behavioral psychologist of today B.F. Skinner, scorn politics because there is an earthly "way," there is a solution to all the problems that politics deals with so badly and at so much human cost. Whether they have a free anarchist community or a behaviorally engineered utopia in mind, they urge us to ignore conventional politics while concentrating on preparation for the politics-free society.[6]

Finally, there are those who reject politics because it is just another trivial human activity, meaningless before the eternal verities and cycles of *nature*. They place politics against nature and see it as degrading in comparison with the grandeur and inspiration of nature. We think at once of Thoreau at Walden, on the Merrimac or at Cape Cod, and relive his immortal words of celebration of the glories of a natural world he knew so well. We recall his angry words of protest over the follies and futilities of human politics.[7]

These antipolitical stances not only share the belief that politics is a secondary concern, but they also agree on the proposition that politics is ordinarily dangerous. After all, if God, Utopia, or Nature is what really matters, then any interest we show in politics is ultimately a diversion of our minds and energies from what we should care about. It is a snare and a temptation that can lead us astray before we know it.

The eloquence of the opponents of politics echoes throughout the history of human thought, but its force need not lead us to ignore the mundane but significant truth that there is more to life than work, Nature, or even a distant utopia. There are also other people. They count too and they are, indeed, the very heart and marrow of a full and decent life. We must live with them as a practical matter and we hope to live well with them as an ideal. We repeat our earlier point: politics is the way in which we can and must regulate our lives together. It can be a potential mechanism for helping each other. It can even be a means for human growth. It operations may be imperfect or worse, yet, if we ignore it, we doubt that our inevitably collective life will improve. If politics is usually not the highest of human enterprises, so it is scarcely the least worthy.

We need it even if it is of restricted use in our complex world. The alternative is

[6]B. F. Skinner, *Walden Two* (Macmillan: New York, 1948).
Lao-Tzu, *The Book of Tao* (New York: Peter Pauper Press, 1962).
L. Tolstoy, *The Kingdom of God is Within You* (New York: Noonday Press, 1961).
[7]H. D. Thoreau, *Walden and Other Writings* (New York: Random House, 1950).

to surrender any aspiration that through public interaction we may grow together. It is also to surrender to the few who do care about politics the power to determine that side of our existence that politics will control.

III

ORGANIZATION VERSUS ANARCHY

Anarchists indict all forms of the state as we have known it, an organized political community especially distinguished by a government with coercive powers. They attack the state and government with more vehemence than they shower on informal political arrangements. Their denunciations raise the vexing and age-old question in political philosophy: Is the existence of the state and government morally defensible? We tend to take their necessity and moral appropriateness for granted, even though we may not like one or another form of the state. Yet it is an error to *assume* that government is a good idea in human affairs without carefully evaluating anarchist ideas.

Anarchic viewpoints are not uniquely modern. In classical Athens, the Cynic Diogenes took an anarchical view of the state, denied the need for it, and also challenged all of its claims of legitimacy. While it can be found in all periods of history, anarchism had its most extensive appeal in the nineteenth century, producing such diverse spokesmen as the Russian Peter Kropotkin and the American Henry David Thoreau. In the recent New Left period of the late 1960s, there was another burst of sympathy for the anarchist perspective that resulted in one especially trenchant defense of anarchism among many, Robert Paul Wolfe's *In Defense of Anarchism*. There seems to be every evidence that in differing times and places the anarchist view will inevitably reemerge and pose its troubling accusation that all governments and nation states are as dispensible as they are immoral.[8]

The cornerstone of the anarchistic attack on the state and government and other centers of power is the assertion that each is deeply unethical in its very nature. Anarchists assert that all states and governments necessarily negate or at least limit individual rights and personhood. For them people and their right to pursue self-chosen objectives without interference is the supreme value. On the other hand, governments are about laws, regulations, taxes, and traffic lights, all of which are designed to restrict the individual and do so time and again all too effectively. Anarchists maintain that the only conclusion from this fact is that

---

[8]P. Kropotkin, *Mutual Aid* (New York: McClure, 1907).
H. D. Thoreau, *Civil Disobedience* in *Walden and Other Writings*, op. cit.
R. P. Wolff, *In Defense of Anarchy* (New York: Harper & Row, 1970).

governments cannot be justified. They are tyrannical and deprive people of their intrinsic free and cooperative spirits.

Many people readily agree with anarchists when they observe dictatorships or tyrannies in action. These governments surely block the individual at every turn. Many agree also when it comes to less authoritarian but still highly elitist or oligarchic states. Yet most of us want to make an exception of supposedly democratic regimes grounded in the free consent of individuals who constitute or sustain democratic governments. It is at this juncture that anarchists most strongly insist that *all* governments, including allegedly democratic ones, curtail individual freedom. Wolff, Thoreau, and Kropotkin all maintain that majority rule means turning over to the majority or its agents in the political system the right and the power to decide what is best for each of us. Tyranny of the majority is still tyranny to its victims. It takes away from every individual his ultimate authority to rule over his or her own life. They insist that beneath the trappings of democracy lies the enduring reality that in theory and practice democracy involves the surrender of individual sovereignty. Nothing could be more immoral.

If we share the anarchist's concern with individual liberty, as most of us do, it becomes obvious that anarchism makes a powerful moral objection to states and governments. They are indeed restrictive and coercive like other institutions. There is an exaggeration here, however, that is important to explore. Anarchists have a tendency to be monistic in their virtual obsession with personal freedom, whereas there are other values worth pursuing. For example, we might want to have security of our person and property. Many people would say that this is as vital as individual freedom and argue that only (the right kind of) government can provide security. Everybody in life has to accept a balance among the many values they wish to maximize. Liberty is not the only objective most persons want, and they give up a good deal of it in order to gain security, among other things.

Even if we did all support the anarchists' sympathy for radical freedom above all else, it is still not clear that we would choose to have no state. Unless we are tremendously optimistic about human capacity for voluntary cooperation and for the avoidance of conflict, we may doubt that anarchy will be a condition that is nearly as fruitful for freedom as it might be for the tyranny of a few strong humans over the many weak. We may suspect that the absence of government might bring as much chaos as consensus.

A second anarchist argument concentrates on the irrelevance of past history in estimating future possibilities for anarchistic achievement. Anarchists declare that the fact that the state has been a central part of human experience in almost all known history does not prove we could not do without it. Nor does it establish that governments are at all ethical. After all, murder is an inescapable part of the human story, but this fact neither proves that we must have murder in the future nor convinces us that murder is a good thing. Anarchists charge that statists suffer from a twin error. They lack sufficient confidence in human possibilities under better conditions in the time ahead and they frequently, if erroneously, confuse what exists or has existed with what is right.

Certainly the anarchists are correct in pointing out that there is no necessary connection between what is ethical and current practice. However, unless there is a great deal more research that yields convincing evidence that it is coercive institutions that cause people to be uncooperative, the lack of past anarchic communities (except for some small-scale experiments) gives pause to a naive acceptance of anarchist claims in this regard. At the very least, much more evidence needs to be accumulated before we are entitled to make firm conclusions.

A third and completing dimension to the anarchist case consists of the anarchist proposition that, despite what many believe, government is not a practical way to regulate human affairs, especially since there is a feasible alternative available. Anarchists ask: What is so practical about government? What does it do for people that is so wonderful and indispensable? As anarchists read the record, the legacy of the state is an account of unrelieved human exploitation, robbery, murder, and denial of human liberty and creativity. They point to the world's slums, to the ever-spiraling crime rate, to wars, to concentration camps, and to prisons. Everywhere they look they see the denial of the human spirit accomplished under a fake banner that proclaims the so-called benefits of government. They claim that people react to tyrannical, organized oppression by adapting to it, by being oppressive and violent.

The anarchist says that there is another, better, way that is surprisingly practical. Most anarchists from Kropotkin to Robert Paul Wolff never shared Thoreau's conception of anarchism as a lonely, purely individualistic journey. They say that human beings, when they are freed from the stunting oppression of governments and police, will come together in cooperative communities, working and living in harmony as social individuals. When freed from hostile competition, people recognize their basic commonality and this leads to solidarity and cooperation. For them, free cooperation is the pragmatic answer to impractical government.

This anarchist vision is attractive. But the stance of those who accept the necessity of government cannot be ignored because it is called into question. Despite their protestations, anarchists seem a bit too confident about the possibility of finding an alternative to the state. To be sure, there are cooperative as well as competitive aspects of the human personality, but the anarchist vision of an automatically cooperative society once coercive institutions are done away with is as open to doubt as the faith of the conservatives that humans function best in a rigid hierarchy. Government can be good or bad, coercive or liberating. It serves as an agency for conflict resolution in areas of public policy involving group conflicts and it can allocate resources of public need as easily as it can bully, make war, and suppress minorities. The record of organized governments in this or any other matter contains both kinds of governmental behavior. Instead of condemning (or accepting) states as a whole, we feel it is more appropriate to realize that large-scale organizations, although valuable, are coercive and to ask whether that coercion can be minimized. It may help to reduce coercion by remembering the anarchist critique of the state.

The more realistic anarchists insist that a combination of intense education and powerful social pressure can replace police and jails. They do not rely on a chimerical goodness of humanity. They argue that a society that has an ongoing and rigorously maintained consensus needs nothing else to maintain its integrity and safety. They may be right, but the result is hardly coincident with the classic anarchist objective of expansive human choice. In a very real sense, these communities may not have an organized government, but they will be trading the prospects of a social tyranny for a political one. Neither is desirable, but political institutions are more visible and easier to control than social tyranny.

We must note also the unmistakable and growing complexity of human societies with vast populations and intricate economies. Strong states and active governments can and do assist in directing and controlling this complexity. It is questionable whether a decentralized anarchist order can manage economic life in the populous modern age without dismantling productive orders at a high cost in terms of the average standard of living. Nor is it entirely clear how an anarchist society could handle all the welfare functions that modern governments increasingly assume. In a world of sharply reduced gross national product, where would the means be found to aid the old, the sick, and the blind? Moreover, recent experience in famine-ravaged lands of Africa and South Asia suggests that even basic human survival may be sacrificed where there is no efficient government to provide basic services in the absence or failure of private means.

We cannot easily get away from the state. It is a viable if not reliable means toward helpful, responsive social life. But there can be no other defense for the existence of a state than its record of practical accomplishments. As a means its test is what a government does for us. The immense value of the anarchist position is that it reminds us that government is no automatic or divine good, nor is its record of performance, now and in the past, always a flattering or reassuring one. We frequently need organized government as a practical matter, but we also must heed the anarchist warning that it carries frequent dangers with it.

IV

WHO SHOULD RULE? BY WHAT CRITERION?

Who should rule? Who has the moral right to rule? History contains an unending record of human struggle over this fundamental question of politics and political theory. Once government exists this problem is inevitable. Consider all the wars that have been fought over this issue, the revolutions under-taken, the lives lost (or "given"), as humans contested the right to govern. From beginnings of written records to the latest African coup, the struggle to establish authoritative leadership is a perennial one.

This section of the chapter investigates this problem, what is often called the problem of legitimate authority, exploring several of the many viewpoints that thinkers over time have had about who should rule. Each perspective contains two inseparable parts. One describes who should rule while the other names the qualification or criterion by which the ruler's legitimate authority is maintained. The crucial matter is the second part, the qualification for legitimate authority. One qualification or another can justify several, if not all, answers to the query of who should govern. For example, if the appropriate standard for legitimate authority is popular consent, then one could support a host of quite different democratic systems under that rubric, anything from participatory government to the quite elitist rule of an elected few. It could include the New England Town Meeting, Britain's elitist prime ministerial rule, or Lenin's Democratic Centralism. On the other hand, if a standard of consent is used that demands considerable direct manifestation of support, perhaps no government in the world today would pass muster.

The vital issue for political theory, then, is not so much who rules as by what authority may anyone rule, the problem of legitimacy. What conditions give governors, whoever they are and whatever form of government they constitute, an ethical right to exercise power? By what values do particular polities claim moral validity?

The most popular, if not the sole standard of legitimate authority, is the democratic one. According to it, governments are legitimate only when they receive and retain the consent of the governed. Just how much consent through what forms of participation is necessary to establish legitimacy is debated within the democratic camp. Most democrats agree that popular endorsement that consists of little more than genuine or forced roars of popular approval at mass rallies or choiceless elections is not enough, partly because they do not open sufficient alternatives to the populace. In the United States, for example, there are elections with at least some range of choice, but some critics wonder whether consent exists through regularized elections when 40 percent or so of the adult population does not bother to vote for president. On the other hand, the Tanzanians claim that a one-party election can be sufficiently democratic. These disputes lead to questions. How often should elections be held? How much choice provides an adequate range of choice? Must there be plenty of opportunity to leave the country and find haven elsewhere in order to have consent to stay to have meaning? These are hard problems that explain why there is so much disagreement among those who are able to unite on the broad notion of democratic legitimacy. (We will consider consent further in Chapter 7, on political obligation.)

Democrats do not agree, either, on what support a democratic criterion of authority may rest. Some, such as the contemporary philosopher, John Rawls, argue that because we are all moral equals as persons, we may play an equal role in approving who rules us. Others talk, as Thomas Jefferson did, in terms of natural rights, maintaining that we all have the right by nature to approve who shall govern us. Still others declare that everyone is more or less wise, certainly wise enough to choose who should exercise power over them, and a society is wrong as well as foolish to ignore what we may call this right of common wisdom. All of these justifications stipulate that the foundation of legitimacy must be the honor and respect that we owe every person. This is what democracy has always been about.

They all tend to argue also that the same rough equality that justifies instituting a political system based on the consent of the governed supports the provision of rights of opposition. All opinions must be considered, aspiring alternative rulers be available and elections open to genuine contest. It is clear that governors elected without opposition cannot easily be said to have gained the authentic consent of the governed, for perhaps an opponent would have defeated them.

Finally, it is worthwhile making the point again that the supporters of the democratic principle of proper authority, like all others, have no single opinion about the form of government, in this case the type of democracy, that may legitimately exist in one nation or another. The problem of which form of a democratic state is best treated as a separate problem whose complexities we consider in the next section.

The second side of the case for a democratic notion of legitimate authority comes from the weaknesses of competing resolutions of the dilemma. Another conception, for example, argues that tradition provides proper authority. This perspective is dominant in past and present tribal societies where rulership is grounded in practices that are taken for granted and seem to originate in the indefinable past. Yet almost all stable societies depend on this version of legitimacy to some degree, even though few "modern" societies make it the linchpin of just authority. Certainly in the United States or England the ways in which the president or king is inaugurated are highly traditional. The historical familiarity attached to the four-year process of a presidential term helps us feel that the present is linked to the past—and all is well. The rich tradition that surrounds American independence—the drafting of the Constitution by the "Founding Fathers," the defense of the union by Lincoln, and so on—all constitute a tapestry of history that is the backdrop of our present-day government and partly sustains it through traditions. This process is evident in many other nations, including Canada, Mexico, and Greece.

The greater the role tradition plays in defining the just authority of a political order, the more likely that system will resist changes. Indeed, to the traditionalists, change is a principal enemy, for each change brings a break with the sacrosanct past. Edmund Burke, the great eighteenth-century traditionalist, argued that we ought to preserve the main outlines of what we have because they were proven in the past. If we did not let tradition govern us, we would have a dictator or a majoritarian mob, both of them frightening tyrants. Neither of these options could possibly match the practical wisdom of humanity over the centuries that created our current political forms. Nor did Burke think the massive changes sought by radicals in the French Revolution would endure in a regime likely to be a stable form of order. Old habits would not be swiftly displaced by new-fangled ideas of reformers. Modern traditionalists agree.[9]

In the traditionalist outlook, then, there is a deep sense that the past is wiser than the fleeting notions of the present, whether interpreted by rulers or majorities. While the implication here is that the traditionalists are both conservative and antidemocratic, this is not always true, for traditionalists may support any form of *stable* government, from rule by tribal chieftan to governance by the British Parliament *as long as* each state respects its own nation's traditions and is congruent with them.

Tradition does have its stabilizing, practical purposes for almost all societies, but as a moral form of authority it is flawed. Traditionalism flounders when it tries to support its guiding proposition, that what has been done or justified in the past is moral for today. One may make a utilitarian case for this supposition as Burke did by stressing its practical stabilizing benefits, but then every aspect of a tradition must be carefully scrutinized to make sure each has positive pragmatic effects. This is a serious and worthy argument, but when tradition is simply accepted as a matter of faith, then it is without foundation as a basis of legitimacy, for it does not follow that just because something has been done in the past it is right to do now. The past is not a moral position. It is a dim fact, but is in no way ethical in itself.

If a traditionalist theory of legitimate authority fails because it confuses an ongoing political order derived from the past with a defense of its legitimacy, a third idea raises quite contrasting objections. The divine or natural law tests of proper authority hold that any government or regime is ruling in a legitimate manner if there is evidence that God (or the gods) or Nature approves. Advocates praise these standards because they are felt to be higher than any others, including traditional ones. They are transcendental norms whose moral sovereignty may scarcely be impuned. Old Testament Israel justified its monarchy under a vision that God's reluctant endorsement of monarchy and His provision of a set of laws made the regime acceptable. Many monarchs even into the last century justified their rule by claiming they had divine right to govern, that God had selected them to exercise authority and denied anyone a right to interfere. Thomas Jefferson, in the Declaration of Independence, assumed that

[9]E. Burke, *Reflections on the Revolution in France* (Indianapolis: Library of Liberal Arts, 1955).

Nature and God were the ultimate standards that applied in any decision as to whether or not a government was legitimate. This was, in fact, a standard view of many of the thinkers of that era on both sides of the Atlantic. Thoreau, too, looked to Nature, to the whistling of the wind in the trees and the free rush of brooks in springtime, when he concluded that Nature decreed that all governments as he knew them were illegitimate.[10]

These criteria of legitimacy are not heard so often in this era of declining faith in God or in Nature. But we should remember that many continue to look to God for guidance in politics as in other aspects of life, while modern-day ecologists appear to be the new prophets of nature, judging governments by their devotion to preserving Nature, although not relying on natural law as a basis for political authority. It is quite impossible to prove that these tests are invalid. Yet, unless we know personally, as a matter of faith, that a particular god or image of Nature is the correct one it is impossible to expect any general recourse to this standard. In the world today it is hard to find much unity on a single transcendental or natural standard of legitimacy and equally hard to get many people even to concede that there might be such a standard. One or another may be our private norm of proper political authority, but few societies, including those in the Third World, can or will use this criterion any more.

We may well regret this fact, and perhaps we should, for without ultimate standards in politics we may seem adrift. But we should not underestimate the human capacity to formulate tentative answers, provisional reasons, existential choices or practical resolutions to guide them in political theory and political life. The only alternatives are not final answers or utter relativism.

One final theory of proper authority focuses on the right of those who have special knowledge to rule. Its proponents, ancient and modern, claim that only experts should direct human society and they maintain that demonstration of the appropriate knowledge earns one legitimacy as a governor. Plato, for instance, contended that Athens would be far better and more legitimately governed if it were controlled by those few who knew what Plato declared to be the Truth. In our age, B. F. Skinner supports a similar ideal—rule by the experts—as his utopia, Walden Two, shows so clearly.[11]

Variations between these two examples, however, reveal the crucial complication attendant to this theory of legitimacy. Many thinkers cling to the standard that only the knowledgeable should govern, but they constantly disagree over

[10]Old Testament, "Kings" and "Chronicles."
The Declaration of Independence.
H. D. Thoreau, op. cit.
[11]Plato, The Collected Dialogues, E. Hamilton and H. Cairns, Editors, (Princeton, N.J., Princeton University Press, 1961).
B. F. Skinner, Walden Two, op. cit.

what knowledge sanctifies legitimacy. Skinner's behavioral managers have a certain form of psychological knowledge and skill that he contends is the proper bulwark for their authority to lead their community. The knowledge that Plato considers essential for his guardian rulers is quite another type of knowledge, knowledge of the transcendent forms of truth and morality, the ultimate and objective rules of the universe. In the face of disputations over who is truly wise enough to govern, we must hesitate before following any one of the claimants to special knowledge in the realm of politics, whether they are astrologists, natural scientists, social scientists, or clergymen. We may doubt their legitimacy because we have no reason to accept one or another of their assertions of expertise.

Aristotle provided another, equally powerful, reason for rejecting the linkage of one form of expertise or another with political legitimacy. He challenged anyone to demonstrate to him that in matters of basic public policy any citizen, however wise in whatever ways, knew more than anyone else what is best for him. His analogy that only someone who wears a shoe knows whether or not it fits is still a powerful, indeed decisive, argument against the view that expertise should confer legitimacy. Aristotle did not mean that there should not be temporary governors or public officials nor do we suggest that some technical matters may not be best directed by experts. Instead, his point and our point is that it is simply impossible to prove that anybody knows what is best for us in a better way than we do.[12] We all are experts about ourselves and each of us has the same stake in our political community. (See the discussion in Chapters 4 and 5 on liberty and equality.)

There are other versions of just political authority, but these four—consent, tradition, transcendent norms, and expertise—are most serious. Our view is that consent, which involves a notion of participation also, is the most convincing. It is a doctrine that holds that respect for every person requires a form of political authority that is based on the consent of the governed. This is the essence of democratic authority: no state is legitimate that does not use the participation and opinion of its citizens and thus exists for the needs of its citizens and not vice versa.

This democratic view is widely shared in the world today, of course, so much so that a UNESCO study not too long ago showed that almost all states asserted that they were democratic. Even if we insist that there can be no genuine consent without regular channels for the expression of consent (or denial of consent), many nations still would pass the test, although the majority would not, and thus may be considered, to some extent, democratic. Nor does it do away with the vast number of conflicting opinions over what democracy *at its best* would be like. This is discussed in Chapter 3.

[12]Aristotle, *The Politics* (New York: Oxford University Press, 1962).

SUGGESTIONS FOR SUPPLEMENTARY READING

On Politics

Berelson, B., P. Lazarsfeld, and W. McPhee, *Voting* (Chicago: The University of Chicago Press, 1954).
Thoreau, Henry D., *Walden and Other Writings* (New York: Random House, 1950).
Crick, Bernard, *In Defense of Politics* (Chicago: The University of Chicago Press, 1962).

On Organization and Anarchy

Wolff, Robert Paul, *In Defense of Anarchy* (New York: Harper & Row, 1970).
Thoreau, Henry D., *Civil Disobedience,* many publications.
Camus, Albert, *The Rebel* (New York: The Vintage Press, 1956).

Who Should Rule?

Aristotle, *The Politics,* many publications.
Burke, Edmund, *Reflections on the Revolution in France* (New York: Library of Liberal Arts, 1955).
Jefferson, Thomas, *Notes on the State of Virginia,* many publications.
Plato, *The Republic,* many publications.

Concepts of
Democracy

WHAT FORM OF DEMOCRACY?

Even if it is possible to construct a convincing
case for the principles of democracy as the best kind
of government, how can we decide which of the
many competing types of democracy is the best
one? Democracy means various contrasting things
to various nations and cultures. It undeniably takes
multiple institutional shapes, even if we eliminate
regimes that do not approximate anything we might
call democratic, since they lack elections, political
liberties, checks on abusive power and, in some
cases, everything except the slightest pretense of
honoring the norm of consent of the governed. For
them democracy is the window dressing over the
raw reality of oligarchy and sometimes oppression.
At the very least, however, democracy is a form of
government that institutionalizes public participation in decision making to some extent and involves
the freedom of citizens to get and use political
information so that their public choices will be
informed.

There are four main versions of democracy that
normative thinkers identify today, and they are
clearly the images that have commanded the most
attention in recent years as arguments and counterarguments have swirled around them, as more
and more citizens and theorists have begun to contrast "democracy" as it exists throughout the world
with democracy as they wish it to be.

3

Polyarchy—Pluralism

Perhaps the most widespread form of democracy in the West today, especially within the realm of foreign affairs, is what Robert Dahl calls polyarchy. It is the view that democracy may best be understood as requiring universal suffrage among adults, selection by voters from among two or more contending groups of elites who seek to govern, and provision for extensive political liberties and formalized mechanisms for opposition within a regularized constitutional framework. It is the epitome of the modern, Western version of democracy as representation of citizens rather than mass participation.

Many political scientists believe that this form of governing, especially in foreign affairs, is what many governments and citizens mean by democracy (even though they do not use Dahl's label to describe their view). It certainly appears to be close to the view that recent American presidents, from Kennedy to Ford, have taken of democracy, especially as they operated in the realm of foreign affairs. It specifically leaves policy choices to the elite rulers, while reserving to the public periodic selection among these elites. People do not govern under polyarchy, they merely choose their governors. It gives leaders considerable leeway and legitimacy as long as they regularly ask for approval at stated intervals.

This concept of democracy has been slow in developing as a formal theory, despite its long-lived health within states describing themselves as democracies. It was really not until after World War II that Dahl and others began to describe and defend the polyarchic sides of Western nations within the framework of democracy. Before then, it had been assumed from the days of classical Greece to Jefferson that democracy could not include so much elitism and so little citizen participation as has become increasingly the norm in Western polities.

Proponents of polyarchy suggest that it provides the usual necessities for democratic government, such as representation—thus legitimacy—as well as regularized checks on the necessary rulers. But their emphasis generally has been upon three particular advantages which they maintain polyarchy possesses. First, they praise polyarchy as a functional form of democracy. Second, they insist it reflects a mature reaction to the lessons about human behavior taught by modern social science as well as the "totalitarian" experiences of World War II. Third, they argue that polyarchy promotes long-term stability better than any other form of governance. These propositions are important and we need to examine them in some detail.

The first point, that polyarchy is a functional type of democracy that can work in the concrete situations of the modern world, has two dimensions. One stresses that polyarchy is functional because it provides for a division of labor that is absolutely essential in modern industrial and technological societies. Life has grown so complex now that it is simply not possible and would be a drastic error to have each citizen involved in major policy decisions. Consequently, it makes sense to have a relatively few people whose primary activity is government just as long as there is an ultimate control over them through a competitive electoral process. Another part of the functional case for polyarchy is the contention that only polyarchy takes adequate account of the vast numbers of citizens who inhabit contemporary states. Sheer numbers makes it unrealistic to attempt to increase the kind and degree of participation beyond what polyarchy offers. It is asserted that only small groups can debate and discuss policy issues without falling under the sway of the demagogue or of emotion. Meeting with thousands, not to say millions, does not even seem physically possible unless the word "meeting" becomes hopelessly stretched out of rational shape. Overall, the conclusion that many democratic theorists in our age reach is like that of Giovanni Sartori, who states that "distrust and fear of elites is an anachronism" in our complex populous age.[1]

Many political scientists, including Dahl and Sartori, note another feature of polyarchy that they believe makes it the best democracy we can get. They claim polyarchy is the only form that is congruent with what we now know about human behavior in politics. They report the avalanche of findings in modern social science research in the past thirty years, such as the landmark study, *The American Voter*, much of which shows that the average American citizen has only a minimal interest in the political process, has surprisingly little information about it, and is prepared to devote scant time to becoming more politically interested and informed. This research is usually generalized to extend beyond recent U.S. politics as well. Many thinkers believe that a more participatory system would demand too much time from disinterested and often uninformed average citizens. It would "take too many nights" and interfere with bowling, family, television, or other activities.[2] At their most pessimistic, such theorists of democracy as Schumpeter or Mayo have expressed their disillusion in biting terms, Schumpeter describing the voters as scarcely more "than an indeterminant bundle of vague impulses loosely playing about given slogans and mistaken impressions," while Mayo remarks that "the majority may be brought to agree to any absurdity."[3]

[1]A. Kaufman, "Participatory Democracy" in Connolly, Editor, *The Bias of Pluralism* (New York: Atherton Press, 1969).

   A. Etzioni, "The Fallacy of Decentralization" in T. Cook and P. Morgan, Editors, *Participatory Democracy* (San Francisco: Canfield Press, 1971).

   R. Dahl, *After The Revolution?* (New Haven: Yale University Press, 1971), p. 86.

   G. Sartori, *Democratic Theory* (New York: Praeger, 1967), pp. 118–119.

[2]Dahl, op. cit., p. 42.

   Sartori, *Democratic Theory* p. 255.

[3]J. Schumpeter, *Democracy as Elite Competition* in H. Kariel, *Frontiers of Democratic Theory* (New York: Random House, 1970), p. 39.

   H. Mayo, *An Introduction to Democratic Theory* (New York: Oxford University Press, 1960), p. 176 and Chapter Eight.

Yet these theorists do not conclude that democracy must be abandoned. The opposite is the case, since for many of them polyarchy or pluralist democracy offers a way out. It balances nicely the often disinterested and ignorant citizen with a political system in which not a great deal is asked except an occasional vote. At the same time, government proceeds under the actual or potential sway of interested citizens. Elites, whether in power or striving for it, are far more informed and consequently promise to be better leaders than most people could possibly be. The result is a system that provides the legitimacy of consent for an informed minority who want to be in politics, while leaving most people the opportunity to select their leaders undisturbed by any substantial demands of time or energy.

Proponents of polyarchy also maintain that their position deals with the historical experience of totalitarianism, an experience that some believe confirms the suspicion that masses of people can be manipulated remarkably easily in politics. Polyarchy avoids mass action and participation in politics and thus holds down the potential for mass manipulation. Some recent explorers in the world of myth and symbols, such as the political scientist, Murray Edelman, provide sustaining evidence for those who believe there is a great amount of irrational human behavior in politics—activity that surely burst all bounds in Nazi Germany or Stalin's Russia.[4] Enthusiasts for polyarchy assert that its compensations for this inescapable irrationalism in human behavior is the substitution of legitimate and constitutionally checked leadership, thereby avoiding the chance of leaders holding manipulated masses dominated by myths under their thumbs.

The third argument of polyarchalists focuses on polyarchy's supposed ability to harmonize substantial political and social stability with the steady incremental change that every society needs in order to survive in an inevitably changing environment. This supposed advantage of polyarchy is closely connected with the others. Concern over how to deal with extensive populations, the complex order around us in this technological and industrial age, and the marked limitations of the "rational" citizen imply that the polyarchal approach worries a good deal about sustaining an ongoing system and puts a high premium on stability. After all, a more participatory nation would only be one that is subject to voter tempers and tides that could retard effective confrontation of vexing problems of the contemporary age, including maintenance of the social, political, and economic order.

We should not confuse polyarchy with simple defense of the status quo. Thinkers like Dahl have other values besides stability that they undertake to realize in politics, and, in any case, they know quite well that unchanging

---

[4]M. Edelman, *Symbolic Uses of Politics* (Champaign, Ill.: The University of Illinois Press, 1964).

regimes become brittle and dangerously incompetent to master the conflicts and tensions of our time. Change is often supported by polyarchalists. But the changes they seek are variations in elites and policies that proceed within established channels by means of gradual or incremental adjustments. Great radical changes draw no interest from them, for radicalism means a threat to stability and, with it, polyarchal democracy.[5]

Pluralism is a variety of democratic theory that is closely linked to polyarchy. It makes group representation the essence of democratic government. Pluralists hold that groups can effectively carry the wishes of their respective memberships into the corridors of political power and, in domestic affairs especially, the clash of group interests produces as viable a safeguard for the public interest as there can be. The political system of the United States is often cited as an example of a pluralist political system, because of the active role groups play in influencing domestic legislation and its administration. Even our political parties may be seen as collections of groups or interests vying for power and policy influence. But recent studies of other societies show that interest groups are present in some extent in all polities, even those which are the most authoritarian.

Most early American political elites looked with extreme disfavor on interest groups and even on political parties, which they called "factions." Adams, Franklin, Hamilton, and Madison all bewailed the inclination of people to divide into factions because they saw this tendency leading to a republic in which the public good would be sacrificed to selfish interests, especially those of the uneducated commoners. Not all had this view and many did appreciate the apparent, if unfortunate, inevitability of interests operating in politics. Jefferson especially accepted organized parties and interest groups as natural and since his time they have come to be a recognizable and substantial feature of our political life.

While there were thinkers like de Tocqueville in the Jacksonian era and Arthur Bentley in the Progressive era who outlined and defended a theory of pluralism, seeing it as a healthy form of democracy, it was not until after World War II that pluralism received a full-scale exposition and justification as the best type of democracy and its tenets became philosophically integrated with polyarchy. Pluralism became popular among many social scientists, but David Truman's *The Governmental Process* was the classic work on pluralism in action.[6] The rise of interest in pluralism after World War II coincided with the emergence of modern political science and sociology, which sought to look beneath formal and legal governmental institutions to discover the actual rhythms of politics. When political scientists and sociologists did investigate "actual" politics, what they found was the reality of pluralism in the United States, Britain, and other

[5]This is even true in Dahl, op. cit.
[6]D. Truman, *The Governmental Process* (New York: Alfred A. Knopf, 1951).

countries, a reality with which they were often highly satisfied. They often felt no need to explore democratic theory any further.

Pluralists advance three key propositions that they believe support their vision of a democratic polity. They argue first that only pluralism guarantees representation that is as meaningful as is possible in the contemporary world. Pluralism allows citizens organized in groups an input into the political decision-making process that goes beyond polyarchy's competitive elections. It permits groups to represent their constituents in the ongoing, day-to-day legislative and administrative policy-making process. At the same time, pluralists say that pluralism takes account of the facts that so worry polyarchalists: people's limited interest and time for politics, intricate societies and governments, and mass populations. Pluralism provides a form of democracy that neither depends heavily on the rationality of the average citizen nor ignores the need for leadership and centralization. It provides for a large number of intermediate-level leaders in the dress of group heads and their lobbyists who have the time, interest, and expertise to overcome the barriers to representation in our political system.

Pluralists also believe that their ideal for government is most representative because the configuration of conflicting interests that constitutes a pluralist system ensures that all perspectives will be heard. If they form a group everybody can have their say, everyone can be represented. Pluralists also presume that everyone can join or form a group that will be *influential* as well as merely *heard*. This is an important—and controversial—claim.

Second, pluralists defend their ideal because they say that it is a practical form of democracy. They contend that a theory of democracy that is impossible to achieve is of no help in the hardheaded world of politics. Pluralists note that citizens operate in politics less as individuals than as members of groups. Politics simply is about the clash of group interests. They also observe that it is rare when individuals get much accomplished in the political process, whereas groups have the muscle to get results. Ralph Nader is significant more as an exception than as a rule—and even he has a growing organization backing him up. Pluralists argue that since politics is about group life and effective political action, we must accept that this is the reality that describes how democracy flourishes. Because pluralism is, above all, about group representation, it is alleged to be a practical conception of democracy, well suited to the living texture of politics.

Third, pluralists argue that their system can provide the optimum balance of stability and change that we can expect from any political order. Pluralists are confident that conflict between groups that is contained within well-understood rules of the game will normally produce compromises that both provide continuing support for pluralism and achieve gradual alterations that a political system can handle without turmoil. They react angrily to those who scoff at compromise as a denial of everybody's personal preferences and principles. They reply that only pluralist compromise will give us some of our objectives in a framework where others get partial satisfaction too, guaranteeing reasonable stability. However, it is not at all clear that pluralism has a monopoly on the ability to produce compromise. "Gentlemanlike" rules of the game can be sought and institutionalized in any political community if it satisfies the needs and aspirations of most of its citizens.[7]

Participatory Democracy   The language of politics records the perennial ideal of participatory democracy. Many terms flow from an impulse toward participatory democracy: decentralization, community control, localism, even federalism. In the last decade this old impulse and these seasoned words have undergone a revival that is as famous as it is controversial. The American black power cry for "community control," community action agencies, and poverty program experiments in decentralization, agitation for police review boards, and decentralized educational systems, New Left slogans for "power to the people," students and workers in the streets of Paris with demands, Tanzanian Ujaama, or George Wallace's celebration of local decisions by plain folks all remind us of the myriad dimensions of interest in participatory and decentralized politics. Nor should we forget the leading social scientists who have argued against participatory politics along with some political philosophers who support it who have together created a debate of considerable intensity.

Enthusiasts of participatory democracy consider it the ideal as well as the most practical form of democracy. Its central premise is that all of us should decide directly in an assembly, or its nearest functional equivalent, what policies and leaders, if any, we wish to have. Participatory democrats do not understand how democracy can be said to exist except when citizens are in actual control over their lives. Certainly, they say, democracy is dead when we have surrendered our power of self-government to polyarchal elites, "representative" legislatures or aggressive interest groups. Many primary democrats grant a need for central governments as well as national elections to legitimate national leaders, but they seek to minimize this aspect of political reality and to decentralize power and authority as much as possible.

Arguments for the moral validity of participatory democracy extend back at least to classical Greek days. Moreover, as the bitter critiques of Athenian participatory government by Plato and others indicate, primary politics had enemies from its beginnings as well.[8] Among great political theorists of the past who praised the participatory ideal in terms of its value as a style of government, Rousseau, Jefferson, John Stuart Mill, and John Dewey deserve the most note

[7]R. Dahl, *Pluralist Democracy in the United States* (New York: Rand McNally, op. cit.
[8]F. J. Frost, Editor, *Democracy and The Athenians* (New York: Wiley, 1969).
   Plato, *The Republic*, F. Cornford, Translator and Editor (New York: Oxford University Press, 1945).

today. All, however, agreed that modern conditions foreclosed any possibility of recreating classical Athens, and all pointed to factors such as numbers, territory and human social characteristics that made complete participatory government, Rousseau's "government of the gods," unlikely. But all of these theorists considered vastly expanded citizen involvement to be synonymous with good government and eminently practical as well. In the end, they shared Pericles' and the Athenian democrats' faith that living democracy was participatory democracy.[9]

Since primary democrats pose the most serious contemporary challenge to the established polyarchy-pluralist definitions of democracy, consideration of participatory politics requires a considerable discussion in order to indicate what many of the main points of dispute have been among the contending visions of democracy in our age. The participatory school begins, like its competitors, by claiming to personify the highest possible standard of representation. Primary democrats claim that the fullest imaginable, most accurate, and most immediate type of representation is small scale and personal in nature—in a word, direct. They feel that representation is a hollow substitute for personal, meaningful participation in governmental affairs. Only direct representation can make political institutions responsive in performance as well as name. They ridicule the polyarchal position, maintaining that polyarchy is merely the principle of elective monarchy, a standard which provides no representation on issues and precious little in regard to leadership selection. They claim that, once elected, a polyarchal elite is free to dictate its will until it has to be on its best behavior in order to win the next election. In like fashion they dismiss pluralist protestations about group representation, noting that few groups really speak for their mass members as often as they do for their well-insulated elites. Participatory democrats also point out how many people (especially the poor and disadvantaged)[10] have no group to pressure and lobby for their interest.

Polyarchal and pluralist thinkers, however, dispute the idea that community control is uniquely democratic or representative. They cite the lack of democ-

---

[9] J. S. Mill, *Representative Government in Utilitarianism, Liberty and Representative Government* (New York: E. P. Dutton and Co., 1951), pp. 209 and 305.

D. Lilienthal, *Democracy on the March* (New York: Pocketbooks, 1945).

W. Agard, *What Democracy Meant to the Greeks* (Madison, Wis.: The University of Wisconsin Press, 1960).

J. Dewey, *The Public and Its Problems* (Chicago: Swallow Press, 1954).

[10] A. Altshuler, *Community Control* (New York: Pegasus, 1970).

P. Bachrach, *The Theory of Democratic Elitism* (Boston: Little, Brown and Company, 1967).

M. Berube and M. Gittell, Editors, *Confrontation at Ocean-Hill Brownsville* (New York: Praeger, 1969).

Cook and Morgan, *Participatory Democracy*, op. cit. C. Hamilton and S. Carmichael, *Black Power* (New York: Random House, 1967).

H. Kariel, Editor, *Frontiers of Democratic Theory*, op. cit.

C. Pateman, *Participation and Democratic Theory* (Cambridge: Cambridge University Press, 1970).

racy in many small towns dominated by well-established elites and they report the findings of small-groups studies that do not sustain the participatory democrats' vision of an equalitarian and free democracy. They continually return to their belief that leadership is a permanent feature in human affairs. However, there is no definitive body of evidence proving the case for either side of this particular dispute. Much more research is needed.

Moreover, polyarchal theorists like Dahl remain convinced that participatory politics concentrates too exclusively on the value of heightened democracy without appreciating sufficiently that other values must be balanced with democracy. Dahl calls attention to the importance of efficiency, and it is a widespread belief of those democrats opposed to participatory politics that it is hopelessly inefficient as an instrument for a successful, functional government. Their views about leadership may be explained from this perspective also. They insist that leadership provides a vital embodiment of the practical principle of division of labor and that it is especially necessary in order to sustain an efficient government in a world where there are more and more involved and highly structured social and technological arrangements.[11]

This objection may seem legitimate, but is is much less a problem for many participatory democrats than critics assume. Many advocates of primary government are prepared to sacrifice a good deal of efficiency. They do not value efficiency for its own sake nearly as highly as their critics do. Robert Paul Wolff, for instance, admits that primary democracy would not result in a technically efficient society in the short run. But he continues to argue for participatory democracy, challenging the notion that efficiency is all important. The potential quality of institutions rather than how efficiently they might work excites the participatory democrats. Wolff, like other participatory democrats is willing to trade some efficiency for such values as liberty and equality that will serve to justify government on moral grounds as well as supposedly practical ones.[12]

Another side of the polyarchal position on efficiency focuses on the chance that localism may frustrate a broader national will, may be quite undemocratic from a national perspective. National majorities may be overruled by local majorities that may not always be particularly kind or fair in their treatment of their own local minority. Polyarchalists question, for example, whether a powerful participatory system in the U.S. deep South might not allow bigots to flaunt national civil rights laws with impunity creating a form of tyranny over local blacks or whether the factional hatreds associated with the Nigerian civil war might not be exacerbated by local control. Perhaps, indeed, institution of participatory politics would mean that public policy would be governed entirely

---

[11]Dahl did not retreat from this position even in *After the Revolution,* op. cit.

[12]G. Almond and S. Verba, "The New Polity" in Kariel, *Frontiers of Democratic Theory,* op. cit., p. 59.

R. P. Wolff, *In Defense of Anarchy* (New York: Harper, 1970).

by local majorities. However, any kind of democracy as a form of government is not a social panacea—it cannot erase cultural misunderstanding or change history. At best, it can allow a framework for consensus to grow.

Participatory democrats claim, with good reason, that the size of a government is not a guarantor of tyranny or its absence. They believe a smaller, more responsive participatory democracy may be no worse in regard to majority tyranny, *ceteris paribus,* and much better at the translation of public opinion into policy. Certainly, no form of democracy, be it polyarchal or primary, can easily solve clashes between majorities and minorities, a problem that will be dealt with more fully in Chapters 4 and 5, "Liberty and Equality," I and II.

Participatory democrats, then, feel that the potential benefits outweigh the possible risks of attempting primary government, or at least a drastic return of power from central to community governments. They appreciate that most societies all over the world appear to be moving toward greater centralization. They know that movement in the opposite direction would represent a gamble. But they feel that we must undertake risks if we are serious about democracy.

The debate over the policy advantages of a more participatory politics via local control has so far not been resolved empirically. But one political scientist, Peter Eisinger, has surveyed the very limited evidence available and he concludes that there is a good deal of reason to be skeptical of uncritical assumptions about policy maximization through control-sharing and primary politics.[13] But the evidence is still meager and many participatory democrats insist that policy questions are not the primary issue. They contend that what really counts is human dignity, which they contend is best served in radically responsive polities.

For example, many black students of community control in the United States find it attractive for reasons beside possible policy benefits. Hamilton and Carmichael, in *Black Power,* argue that community control might accomplish a vast amount for individual blacks just in terms of increased self-esteem: black pride through black power.[14] Most enthusiasts of participatory politics offer this justification for their political theory, a reason which pointedly accents psychological advantages of primary politics. The essence of the argument is that only participatory democracy can develop the human personality: other forms of democracy are merely mechanisms of governance instead of vehicles for human growth.

This has been a long-time theme of participatory democrats. Many traditional theorists starting with Pericles in ancient Athens have claimed that political participation improves, even ennobles, humankind. They have lauded it as the one method of government that breeds the unusually worthy individual. John

---

[13]Peter Eisinger, "Community Control and Liberal Dilemmas" in *Publius, Fall, 1972.*
[14]C. Hamilton and S. Carmichael, *Black Power,* op. cit.

Stuart Mill, Ernest Barker, John Dewey, and David Lilienthal have been among the most exuberant celebrants in the past 150 years, but there have been many.

The exact nature of a politics promoting a more virtuous and developed citizenry is not particularly clear in earlier democratic thinkers. Like their contemporary successors, they are vague about how the "development of human personality" is to take place except by the natural process of free human interaction. The results of the process, however, receive a multitude of descriptions. Participatory government will bring "a spiritual yield . . . a renewed sense that the individual counts" to every person. Each will attain the chance to be truly "human" or realize the "human way of life." People will gain an expanded moral sensitivity, greater "independence of mind" and increased social talents.[15]

This concept of an enhanced personhood in an active community visualized a total experience, making primary democracy in Dewey's words a "way of life." In this framework, the desired individual would emerge. The total process might be complex, but the result would be a new life, a new reality for people, on a plane of achievement and satisfaction never known before.[16]

Most of the literature produced by contemporary social scientists attracted to participatory democracy is in a direct line of descent from these older arguments. Like previous views, it praises the ideal for its potential, which Bachrach describes as "the full development of individual capacities." The literature makes the repeated contention that active participation in an environment that encourages an involved citizen will guarantee a better person.

The hypothesis that psychic good is the best characteristic of primary democracy appears in two modes. There are those who announce the truth of this essentially empirical claim, rather than endeavor to substantiate it. They make multiple, but vague, references to participatory politics as the means to unfold the "intellectual, emotional and moral capacities" of people, or as the guarantee of impressive advances in human "dignity." These objectives are impressive, but there is often scant exploration or explication of what they mean or what their relation is to known empirical data.[17] Some advocates of participatory democracy are considerably more scholarly, however, and deserve to be taken quite seriously. They devote ample attention to the empirical basis for their psychological case. For example, Carole Pateman's *Participation and Democratic Theory* notes a considerable literature that suggests that a sense of personal

---

[15]J. Dewey, "Democracy as a Way of Life" in Kariel, *Frontiers of Democratic Theory,* op. cit., p. 13.

E. Barker, "Democracy as Activity" in Kariel, ibid., pp. 11–12.

C. Pateman, *Participation and Democratic Theory/* op. cit., Chapter Two.

[16]Dewey in Kariel, op. cit., p. 13.

[17]J. Tussman, "The Citizen as Public Agent" in Kariel, ibid., p. 28.

P. Bachrach, *The Theory of Democratic Elitism,* op. cit., pp. 84, 101, 95, and 28.

efficacy, or self-esteem, does tend to develop with involvement in significant areas of life. Other studies reveal that those who take part in specific participatory political situations may attain a greater sense of ego strength even when their participatory institution falls far short of the primary democratic model. For instance, D. R. Marshall's study of a community action board in Los Angeles claims that, even though the experimental effort in participation collapsed in unequivocal failure, the poor who did become entwined in the board's mesh of activity became more self-assured personalities. Daniel Moynihan suggests as well that his experience in the poverty program reinforces belief in this phenomenon.[18]

Another side to the same general argument for the "human" advantages of participatory politics concentrates on the humane values that are supposedly promoted by (as well as manifested in) a participatory society. In particular its proponents suggest that participatory democracy is good when it actually exists because it is a mechanism for community and authentic individualism, and is often a living manifestation of these norms.

The pronounced anarchistic overtones that leap out from the discussions of many of these contemporary radical thinkers are unmistakable; Murray Bookchin writes of "the liberated society" and Herbert Marcuse demands "liberation." Authentic autonomy under an umbrella of broad-ranging freedom is a basic radical-left goal. At the same time, there was and is repeated emphasis on the importance of community. Just as the late Paul Goodman, among others, criticized Western societies for their failure to halt the attrition of freedom in the face of the onslaughts of a remote, bureaucratized state, Marcuse and Robert Paul Wolff have charged that the West has not cared enough for the common good. This charge is heard in the cries of condemnation hurled against neocolonialist elites in the Southern hemisphere as well. The United States, for example, is accused of sacrificing community regard on the altar of egoistic greed as often as Nkrumah was denounced within the African Socialist movement for the same failure.[19]

Most participatory democrats believe that community and individualism are each inextricably linked with the good life; each is valuable because they are part of what makes public life worth living. In addition, they are intimately related to each other; without community there will be no genuine individualism and vice versa.[20]

All these affirmations seem insubstantial indeed to social scientists who are

[18]See Pateman, op. cit.

[19]See R. P. Wolff, *In Defense of Anarchy*, op. cit.
   H. Marcuse, *One-Dimensional Man* (Boston: Beacon Press, 1967).

[20]R. P. Wolff, *The Poverty of Liberalism* (Boston: Beacon Press, 1968).
   L. Sargent, *The New Left: An Introduction* (Homewood, Ill.: Dorsey Press, 1972).
   Bachrach, op. cit., last chapter.

not sympathetic to participatory democracy. They declare that primary democracy is hopelessly impractical whatever the personal or ideological ends it undertakes to realize. Some critics like Henry Mayo acknowledge that participatory politics is abstractly the best form of democracy, while others like Robert Dahl deny this claim, but they agree that participatory democracy in modern societies is an impossible idyll. They express scant patience for a doctrine whose theory, they state, does not accord with the practice of current political systems. They even cast doubt on the participatory nature of the classical participatory ideal of the fifth-century Athens. Robert Dahl goes so far as to brand advocates of participatory politics irrational in their quest for the unrealizable. He charges that "infantile fantasies" have gripped some of these believers in "magic."[21]

These doubts relate quite directly to the political biases of the theorists in question, to the polyarchal concern with efficiency, to the polyarchal-pluralist skepticism about the degree of popular interest and information regarding politics and to their reservations about whether or not increased participation by the masses will bring with it irrationality and even totalitarianism. Bernard Berelson, a social scientist, put it bluntly when he concluded that apathy has much to be said for it in politics.

Many primary democrats acknowledge these doubts, but they reject the idea that the present fears and alarms will necessarily make sense when a more participatory era develops. They believe that people must be given an opportunity to grow and, when they are, they will blossom into responsible, aware, and intelligent citizens. Naturally, they appear ignorant and disinterested today because they are not given a chance. Primary democrats say that by not moving to a politics in which there is a vastly expanded role for individual persons, we only reinforce the negative image—which may be partially real—of the ordinary citizen which pluralist and polyarchal democrats tell us and themselves is the truth. A self-fulfilling prophecy is created in our minds.

A third and final element in the primary democrats' case is their argument that their democracy is open to change and eager for an environment of growth and development. They claim that participatory democracy is confident or at least not negative in its assessment of human nature and ready for whatever alterations time and human enterprise bring. They contrast this confidence with what they take to be the narrow conservatism of polyarchal democracy, a conservatism which they suggest focuses exclusively on the dangers of much change and the glories of stability. They spurn a notion that to them seems pessimistic and even cowardly, while they embrace the idea that life should and will involve risk and change.

[21]H. Mayo, *An Introduction to Democratic Theory*, op. cit., pp. 73 and 41.
   Sartori, *Democratic Theory*, op. cit., pp. 255, 79, 460–461.
   Dahl, *After the Revolution?* op. cit., p. 56.

Polyarchal and pluralist democrats respond by denying the rigidly conservative image that their critics hold about them. They insist that they welcome changes too, but that they want only change that proceeds within an orderly and stable polity. They doubt whether any alterations will be long lived outside of this restraint because of the potential depravity of man unchained. They also feel that primary democrats' enthusiasm about change overlooks the perspective of most people that is much more sympathetic to a familiar and secure environment. Polyarchalists and pluralists return to their theory of incrementalism, which they like so much because it combines modest change with certain stability. They assert that only under the umbrella of an incremental theory of change can the twin, and sometimes competing, goods of change and order be reconciled.

Many of the warnings of polyarchal-pluralist critics of participatory democracy may not be easily ignored. Certainly their pessimism about the human possibilities in politics is not self-evidently absurd. Yet participatory democrats are right to remind us, even if we do not necessarily agree with their conception of democracy, that "realism" and "pragmatism" are not the only perspectives appropriate in politics and may, indeed, lead to self-fulfilling prophecies. The question is not only what works, though a policy that is right must also be able to work, but also which is best.

POPULISM

Another version of democracy is populism, a view particularly familiar to and associated with American history since the nineteenth century. Populist democracy consists of a combination of active majoritarianism and a strong, decisive, central government. It is, in one sense, primary democracy that has made peace with efficiency. This conception of democracy has received some attention in the present day in such books as Newfield and Greenfield, *A Populist Manifesto* and, Fred Harris's *The New Populism*.[22] All populists agree that Western societies have fallen short of representing the majority will, despite their democratic rhetoric, especially in policy matters. They claim that the reality of polyarchy and pluralism has induced us to acquiesce in the ongoing surrender of government to political and interest group elites instead of fighting to have it returned to the people. Populists charge that the cost of our "democracy," with its dimunition of majority will, is stalemate over an entire range of political, social, and economic changes that they feel a majority of citizens would support.

The ancestors of modern populists were the agrarian populists of almost a

[22]Newfield and Greenfield, *A Populist Manifesto* (New York: Praeger, 1972); Fred Harris, *The New Populism* (New York: Saturday Review Press, 1973).

century ago, those American democrats who wanted governmental aid for their problems and who fondly, but incorrectly, believed that a majority in their nation agreed with their demands. Their analysis like that of modern populists identified assorted special interests that they asserted were consciously blocking change and therefore damaging democracy. Populists, among others, were zealous advocates of devices aimed to ensure much greater popular role in decision making, instruments permitting citizens to propose legislation for popular adoption ("initiative") and for requiring popular votes on major policies approved by elected legislatures ("referendum"). They also pressed for acceptance of ("recall") laws to allow citizens to remove elected officials in elections when the majority wanted them removed. Many cities and states retain these populist measures and a good number of modern populists would like to see them become more widespread. Although most populists do not go so far as to embrace direct participation, they feel that representation must be radically improved. They assert that there is no other way to achieve a truly significant popular impact on government.

Populists make two important arguments on behalf of their democratic theory. First, they are confident that populism is at least as democratic as primary democracy and a good deal more so than polyarchy or pluralism. They consider it ridiculous for pluralists to pretend they are democrats, since government by group elites hardly constitutes majoritarianism. Populists dearly hope to see the end of the day when "special interests" rule. On the other hand, they do agree with polyarchal theorists that leadership is important, indeed indispensible, but they suggest that polyarchal elites are scarcely kept in touch with the masses by an occasional election or two. Leaders must be approved frequently by the people and their policies ratified by popular vote in order for democratic legitimacy to exist. Populists do not agree that all representation is tyranny, but rather that typical Western modes of it are fraudulent.

Populists also seek to persuade us that only populist democracy cares about the broad public interest. As the agent for the majority, populist governments would naturally think in general terms about the public good. Populists charge that pluralists endorse a system where everyone is encouraged to think only of their self or group interest. While this opinion overlooks the pluralists who orient themselves to what they describe as the public interest, it is an accurate description of most pluralists who contend that the results of competing interests and interest groups as they appear in governmental decisions and nondecisions *are* the public interest. Followers of polyarchy assert their devotion to the public good as well, but populists dismiss such protestations as a confusion of the public interest with elite desires.

The second aspect of the populists' case is their conviction that populist democracy is a formula for action, for getting things done. In their minds, democracy does not connote delay, equivocation, or stalemate. As far as populists are concerned, the dominant polyarchal/pluralist democracy in many nations proves every day that it is helpless to get a grip on domestic problems. Special-interest groups have so many cozy vetoes over policy that nothing much new can get done. Populists charge that this state of affairs exists in all too many polities, citing the power of oil corporations in the United States, tribal groups in African nations, and trade unions in increasingly impotent Italian governments.

Populists criticize participatory democrats for the same reason. They are not able to get anything accomplished either. Local, participatory government, they suggest, is simply too decentralized and uncoordinated to permit decisive national action to meet crises or to tackle complex national problems. Indeed, many populists suspect that there is already too much community control, while more would only produce a geographic pluralism promising more negative results in the fashion of interest group pluralism.

Some populists sound authoritarian and certainly their emphasis on centralized action may seem more than a little disturbing. But populists insist that strong government authority need not end in despotism. They declare that they approve *only* of a strong government closely responsive to public desires. Thus many populists attack the American record in foreign affairs. They see it as an activism that represents polyarchy in action, an undemocratic leadership operating in an undemocratic manner. They ask, who of us have ever approved a foreign policy?

Their argument for a democratic leadership does not, however, satisfy either participatory democrats or polyarchal pluralists. Primary democrats doubt that populists can depend so much on leadership, while at the same time urging popular participation. They suspect that something will have to go and they expect it to be popular involvement. Their claim is that populists have begged the question in their critique of participatory democracy. The major point is not merely the size of the government but whether there is direct public participation in it. It is an important question that the populists tend to gloss over and their theory is diminished by their refusal to deal with it adequately. Polyarchal-pluralists, on the other hand, regard populist democracy as a danger to every minority. Not only do they forsee majority tyranny, but they fear it will be doubly dangerous since the majority will have a powerful centralized leadership at its command. They contend that democracy means majority rule reconciled with minority rights and they fear for the latter under populism.

Many social scientists also raise the genuine objection that the populist talk about a majority will is no more than a romantic illusion. There is, they say, no majority will on which to build a democracy, only a series of temporary majority coalitions on specific issues and candidates that decay as fast as they develop in the shifting sands of public sentiment. Similarly, they contend, there is no obvious (or hidden) public interest; there are only varying and passing outlooks about what is the public good.

CONCLUSION

The many ideas and issues discussed in this chapter and the preceding one have a common theme: they concern the basic and perennial controversies over what constitutes a legitimate polity in general and what particular institutional variants of it are the best ones. The concept of legitimate and best as we have used them here are not abstractions but refer to basic political values that can and should be maximized by political communities. It is the authors' belief (supported by the preponderance of Western political thought as well as a great deal of nonWestern thought) that the value of human life is the most important one that politics ought to seek to maximize. As we will develop in subsequent chapters, many other values can be derived from this basic one including—but not limited to—political equality, liberty, participation, and justice.

We argue that the state can only be justified if it allows people to relate to each other in a morally acceptable way, that is, if it recognizes the value of human life, and if its institutions and rules provide equality, liberty, and sufficient opportunity for its people to participate in the decisions that affect their lives. These and other parallel values must be assured before the state can *earn* their voluntary political obligation through deed instead of through the use of coercive force. A good state, then, must allow human beings to develop their potentials by serving their needs and desires to accommodate each other. It must never be an end in itself. It must be a means toward a good politics.

Democracy is the form of polity that best approximates that goal. As we have pointed out, democracy includes not solely the modern Western concept of a liberal representative system, but a broad variety of institutional arrangements and values that can be assembled in different ways to form a polity which allows people to participate in political affairs to the extent that they can hold the state liable and responsive to their needs. We agree with C. B. MacPherson that too often discussions of democracy in the West focus exclusively on polyarchy and pluralism or their combination. This is one reason why we have devoted so much effort to an examination of the serious competing claims of participatory democrats and populists. We might have also explored the views of those who see China and Cuba as valid democracies or discussed the idea of British conservative thinkers such as Michael Oakeshott and Patrick Devlin that tradition, representing the accumulation of human experience, is democracy at its best. But we think the debate among polyarchalists, pluralists, populists, and participatory democrats brings out many important aspects of the enduring debate over the nature of democracy to sufficiently introduce the richness of the concept of democracy.

Certainly we argue that democracy, conceived of as the opportunity for regularized popular participation in public decision making, is the ideal (if not perfection) for human government and acknowledge that at the same time it may come in many forms in theory and practice. It cannot be said that it is easy to state explicitly which of even those types we consider is the best. In part, the choice will depend on the circumstances. One of the reasons for the historical variety of democratic regimes from the participatory but restricted citizenship polity of classical Athens to the elitist but universally franchised modern representative versions has been that large and small states, pastoral and industrial ones, and those with an educated versus an uneducated populace have had need for different types of democracy. The need for rapid political and economic development of so much of the Third World requires much more regimentation than is required in the "postindustrial" societies of today. The type of democracy possible and preferable for each will be unlikely to be the same. Moreover, the needs of a polity change as it evolves in time.

Nevertheless, some generalizations are in order. The polyarchalists and the pluralists make their democratic theory too remote and too elite oriented—they do not make individual participation meaningful (which is different from regular) enough to be reliably responsive to public needs. Participatory democracy thought of as radical decentralization, on the other hand, ignores the institutional framework that is necessary to solve the regional, continental, and international problems like ecological policy and war, which encompass areas that are not confined to geographical and political boundaries. Populist democratic theory, too, has as a major flaw its native assumptions about the nature of political problems. It allows only for episodic and spasmodic public participation in such things as referendum, recall, or initiative, which does not make up for the elitist nature of most political institutions. What is more, they give too little attention to problems of minorities in a polity.

In the final analysis, we cannot doubt the populist recognition that government must be able to act effectively in the face of fast-breaking crises. Nor can we disagree with the participatory democrats who claim that where there is little or no meaningful public participation, there is no democracy. Nor do we dissent from the polyarchal or pluralist position that excessive majoritarianism can be costly for the losers within a polity and can endanger civility itself, democracy, and many other values. We conclude that the appropriate unit in any democratic theory should be the individual, not the state or the group. Thus, representative institutions, imperfect as they are at best, should be kept to a minimum, and the maximum possible amount of direct participation that is consistent with efficient mobilization to handle the problems and aspirations of people in a polity should be sought. Where representative institutions are deemed necessary, every effort should be made to keep them responsive to public opinion.

Democracy is basically a method of political interaction as well as a set of institutionalized political values. It needs to be considered in the context of social conditions. It must consider which political values ought to be maximized to bring about the best possible life. If this means that one must be a participatory democrat who is also aware of the problems pointed out by other kinds of democrats and sympathetic to some of the solutions of these problems, so be it. There is nothing wrong in picking and choosing from a variety of informed opinions as a way to develop a concept of a legitimate polity. The result might be a democracy that avoids the radical aspirations of the participatory democrats as well as the satisfied elitism of the polyarchal/pluralists and limits the extreme majoritarianism of the populists. But, if properly conceived and applied, it might be one that could make our polities much more responsive to the individual and much less prone to tyranny. It might become the epitome of legitimacy.

SUGGESTIONS FOR SUPPLEMENTARY READING

Polyarchal and Pluralist Democracy

Campbell, Angus et al., *The American Voter* (New York: Wiley, 1960).

Dahl, Robert, *After The Revolution* (New Haven: Yale University Press, 1971).

_____ , *Pluralist Democracy in the United States* (New York: Rand McNally, 1967).

Edelman, Murray, *The Symbolic Uses of Politics* (Champaign, Ill.: The University of Illinois Press, 1964).

Lowi, Theodore, *The End of Liberalism* (New York: Norton, 1969).

Mayo, Henry, *An Introduction to Democratic Theory* (New York: Oxford University Press, 1960).

Sartori, Giovanni, *Democratic Theory* (New York: Praeger, 1967).

Participatory Democracy

Altshuler, Alan, *Community Control* (New York: Pegasus, 1970).

Cook, T. and P. Morgan, Editors, *Participatory Democracy* (San Francisco: Canfield Press, 1971).

Fantini, M., et al., *Community Control and the Urban School* (New York: Praeger, 1970).

Kariel, Henry, Editor, *Frontiers of Democratic Theory* New York: Random House, 1970).

Pateman, C., *Participation and Democratic Theory* (Cambridge, Eng.: Cambridge University Press, 1970).

Wolff, Robert Paul, *The Poverty of Liberalism* (Boston: Beacon Press, 1968).

Populist Democracy

Hicks, J., *The Populist Revolt* (Lincoln, Neb.: The University of Nebraska Press, 1961).

Hofstadter, Richard, *The Age of Reform* (New York: Vintage Press, 1955).

Newfield, J. and J. Greenfield, *A Populist Manifesto: The Making of a New Majority* (New York: Praeger, 1972).

Liberty and Equality—I

Cries for liberty and equality have resounded throughout history. They have built constitutions and overturned governments. They have etched themselves onto the pages of our political theories. They splash across the front pages of our daily newspapers. Patrick Henry's resistance to British rule was voiced in the cry "give me liberty or give me death!." Jefferson wrote "The tree of liberty must be watered by the blood of tyrants!." During the French Revolution the Parisian masses chanted "Liberty! Equality! Fraternity!" The English political theorist John Stuart Mill wrote a classic essay on the question of liberty. Rousseau, the apostle of community, wrote a discourse on the origins of inequality. In our own age the cries for liberty and equality resound even more loudly. Feminists demand equality. Libertarians attack the welfare state and its bureaucracy. Racial minorities seek equal treatment. Reformers call for maintaining or creating freedom for homosexuals, prisoners, and mental patients.

In this and the following chapter we pursue the topics of liberty and equality. We consider them separately, but we also endeavor to discuss them in relationship to each other. For liberty and equality are as closely linked as any two political values we might name and, in fact, are so intimately intertwined that many theorists view them as being in balance—as one is advanced the other must be diminished. Theorists from Alexis de Tocqueville to John Stuart Mill, from Jean Jacques Rousseau to Albert Camus, have discussed them comparatively. We agree with these thinkers that it makes more sense to view liberty and equality side by side because such comparative analysis fosters an understanding of the nature and limitations of these interdependent political values.

To illustrate from the beginning the depth of the interrelationship of liberty and equality, some examples are appropriate. Our first one is familiar and has generated a great deal of controversy in many communities in recent years. It concerns the sale of a house. From the perspective of the homeowner, it seems fair that the one who paid for the house has the freedom to sell that house to whomever he wants. If he refuses to sell to those of a different color, the owner feels justified in claiming it is nobody else's business. However, let us look at the same situation from the perspective of a potential buyer who is of a different race than the seller. Perhaps the buyer has been a victim of racial discrimination all of his life. He has been forced to live in poor neighborhoods, send his children to substandard schools, put up with inferior municipal services, run increased risks of crime and suffer all of the indignities ghetto dwellers are acquainted with. He wants to buy the owner's house, and he has made enough money to afford it. He feels that it is his equal right as a human being to live wherever he chooses as long as he can pay for it. He is advancing a claim that the liberties of a seller do not extend so far as to permit denial of his right to equal treatment.

Both claims, liberty and equality, have been advanced by different parties, for the same situation, and neither claim can be rejected out of hand as being totally implausible. The problem is that the "twin values" not only arise together with great frequency but that the claims of one or the other are often mutually exclusive. If we grant the claims of one, those of the other party are denied.

The same thing is true of the longtime fight over inheritance laws. Many people object to steep inheritance taxes, arguing that there could be no more basic liberty than the right to make provision for one's children. Yet others contend that equality demands that everyone have an equal chance in life. Yet how can they if the wealthy few are able to give their children the enormous advantage that we all know inherited wealth provides? Or consider a factory owner who maintains that he should have the liberty to produce his products in the freest possible manner, confronted by a government demanding that equal rights of all to a clean environment require him to install costly antipollution devices. The pollution control and safety accessories mandated by the government for our cars constitute a similar example. A buyer might feel that it is his life and his lungs and that he should be free to choose whether to have those extra-cost devices. After all, it is his liberty as a consumer to decide what to buy.

On the other hand, the government has advanced a claim that equal access on the part of all citizens to a livable environment and an equal chance not to be smashed into by some out-of-control death-trap car should take precedence over any consumer liberties.

All of these claims and counterclaims involve serious cases of conflicting liberties and equalities. What is needed is a thorough examination of the definitions and issues involved with liberty and equality, starting with consideration of each concept separately. We begin with liberty.

We tend to associate liberty with choice, specifically with ability to make choices. We commonly assume we are freest when we can choose to do what we will, when we are, so to say, at liberty to do what we want. Freedom in this basic sense is not a thing that we somehow possess, but a condition in which a person lives. Some conditions or situations are free because we can choose in them, others are not because one cannot make any choices.

A proper understanding of what freedom entails is actually a good deal more complicated than this preliminary definition implies, especially when examined in a political context, but this analysis immediately raises a first problem that we must face even though we cannot solve it. Some thinkers, such as the contemporary psychologist B. F. Skinner, argue that we cannot consider any form of liberty because there is no such thing—liberty is an illusion and, therefore, a nonexistent value. We begin our exploration of liberty by asking that most basic of questions: Can it really exist at all outside of our imaginations? Determinists, those who feel that we are not free, believe that our actions are completely fixed by heredity, environment, and other forces beyond our control. If such a full determinist position is accepted, we are not free by definition. In fact, it makes no sense to value liberty at all since we are not responsible for any of our actions, all of which are mapped out for us and are beyond our ability to control.

On the other hand, there are many advocates of the concept that people do have, or can have, considerable liberty. Most political philosophers have agreed that there are areas where individuals can and do make choices that are not predetermined. No two thinkers, no two of us, are likely to agree on how expansive the realm of potential free choice is, or ought to be, for any of us. Some thinkers today, impressed by the factors of environment and heredity edge close to the position of Skinner, while others remain confident that humans have an enormous capacity to determine themselves as autonomous beings exercising free choice.

We do not dishonor a long and still lively tradition of philosophic discourse on the question of determinism and freedom when we argue that the debate seems to us to have an air of unreality about it. We recognize that our conclusion is not universally shared, but we tend to think the question is one that cannot be resolved short of a position of faith. Evidence for each side usually turns out to be disappointingly short of a conclusive proof.[1] Consequently, since we cannot find a definitive answer to the question of whether we are "really" free in a metaphysical sense, or whether it makes sense to talk of "genuine" liberty, we abandon the question by concluding that it does not lead us anywhere for our purposes.

We start instead by assuming that we do have some choice in our lives. We make this particular assumption, as most Western political thinkers have always done because we hope it is true, because we think it is intrinsic to our entire aspiration for humanity, and because we respect the Western image of the individual, one capable of independent action, rational judgment and genuine responsibility. This image of the human person is crucial for our understanding of political morality. Our political theories and our whole ethical thought builds on a concept of an individual who can often choose and often is responsible for his actions.[2] Indeed, if we cannot choose, and are never responsible, then there is no point to considerations of what we ought to do in personal morality or in politics.

Yet we appreciate that liberty is always constrained by natural and environmental factors of all sorts. At one extreme are factors generic to our human species that inevitably limit our potential liberty. This reality is obvious and yet worth considering for a moment. Human beings cannot fly without benefit of airplanes or similar aids, and they cannot be in two places at once. We cannot swim rivers like a fish or outrun our game animals. The list of things we cannot do is almost endless; in fact, it would be much easier to list the things we can do. These natural restraints on our liberty are important because they define the limits to our potential freedom. It makes no difference to us if there is nobody to stop us from soaring like an eagle; we cannot, and therefore can never have any liberty to do so.

Agreement is also widespread that many hereditary or developmental features of every person's unique life circumscribe many choices. Despite modern medicine, few of us can choose to be another sex, or to live forever, or to become children again. Few who are ugly can become beautiful, fewer yet who have no athletic skill can become great athletes, and none at all who have low intelligence can have the liberty to become great intellects.

We suffer substantial limitations as a result of environmental background as well. Obviously, our personal experiences in growing up and in dealing with life's pressures mold and shape us, sometimes in ways we cannot easily overcome, and thereby limit our potential liberty. Beyond this, which takes a toll on each of us, there are certain environmental backgrounds that clearly

[1]Isaiah Berlin has an excellent discussion of these issues and some of their claims and counterclaims in the introduction of his *Four Essays on Liberty* (London: Oxford University Press, 1969).
[2]Ibid.

restrict potential choice more sharply than others. Citizens of a rich country are likely to have substantially more choices available to them than are
those of poor nations just as a suburban child with upper- middle-class parents is
likely to have more freedoms than the average ghetto offspring.

Environmental dimensions of the debate are far more a subject of controversy
than are the factors of nature or heredity. How much are our choices limited by
our background? Consider the classic example of the fight over welfare policies.
Some contend that many people on welfare are not trapped by their personal and
situational environment so much as by their laziness and unwillingness to get out
and work. This viewpoint does not think that environmental determinism is very
strong in this case. Others insist that many on welfare are indeed locked into a
situation, a culture of poverty, which they are helpless to rectify. Such an opinion
reveals considerable belief in environmental determinism.

We do not think that any easy answers to the question of the sway one's
background may exercise in delimiting choices are forthcoming. It seems to us
that there is no profit in following either the persuasion of those who dismiss the
effects of the environment or those who are overwhelmingly impressed with its
chains. Both perspectives are far too sweeping for the detailed and complicated
reality of human experience. We are inclined to say that the amount of potential
freedom one may have will vary from one environmental situation to another.
Only by examining concrete people and environments can one speak with
much confidence about the degree of liberty that is actually available.

Such a process requires that we look not only at the effects of our personal and
cultural background but as well at specific moments of choice and the environmental constraints which they may impose. One intriguing manner of thinking
about this feature of the problem is evident in recent work of Alan Wertheimer.
His view is that even when we agree that a person has the potential for liberty of
choice in a specific situation, when no one cannot say that nature, heredity, or
his background prevent him from exercising his liberty, still he may not be free in
any but a meaningless formal sense.

Wertheimer's insight builds on the undeniable fact that choices have consequences. Sometimes the consequences will be favorable and sometimes they
will not be. However, when the costs of a choice involve serious deprivations for
the person making the choice, it is likely that a person will not make that choice
even though he is not prevented by his heredity or background from doing so,
even though he is technically free to do so. We can, in fact, predict that when
negative consequences are great for choosing to do X, most people will not do
so, hence his term predictive freedom. The exact test that Wertheimer suggests
we should use he formulates as follows: "we want to say that A is unfree . . . to do
X when the likelihood and severity of a deprivation make it *unreasonable* to

expect A to do X." The obvious implication is that even when we appear to be free we often cannot fairly be considered so.[3]

Does all of this mean that we can never be free? As pervasive as these limitations may be, beyond them lies an arena of human personal, social and political experiences. Luckily, the possibilities of action in this arena are so vast that they could easily keep us busy for millenia without there being a danger of exhausting the frontiers of human experience. We still have open a wide range of life-styles, values, and possible political communities. These more than make up for the tangled web of physical limitations, regulations, and cultural patterns that foster pessimism.

However much liberty we may have potentially, our use of any of it immediately leads us to the realm of moral life and social and political philosophy. Those who live alone—hermits—have no need for any concept of liberty other than that which they can observe in nature. They can do what they please unmolested by others; they bother and affect no one by their behavior. Hence their liberty is devoid of moral implication. But most of us are not hermits and do not wish to be. We live our lives in a permanent state of interaction with others. Political communities are places of close social proximity; what we do in them has a reciprocal effect—our actions affect other citizens and theirs affect us. Thus, our freedoms in a polity do have moral implications because of the inseparability of our mutual needs and wants. Our liberty and what we do with it is a subject of moral concern because it influences the quality of life and other political values. In short, while liberty may be abstract as a general concept, in a political community it becomes a moral reality. As such, its meanings and interaction with other values are the proper subject of political theory that deals with moral evaluation and prescription about collective relationships.

Although liberty as a political value has been postulated in literally hundreds of different ways, there are three conceptions that are central to the debate about liberty and that we will analyze extensively to give us a basis of comparison with which to evaluate the varied positions. At one end of the spectrum are positions of those who advocate the greatest liberty and, consequently, have an individualistic focus to their presciptions. At the other end are those who embrace the concept that relatively little liberty is desirable and are, therefore, also advocates of a social bias, collectivism, that seeks to restrict individual freedoms in the interests of the whole political community. A middle position is occupied by those who prescribe less liberty than the individualists but more than the collectivists. This balance between the individual and the community leads them towards a concept of equilibrium when individual and community interests are in conflict within a polity. Thus, the primary index of comparison

---

[3]Alan Wertheimer, *"Is Social Freedom An Empirical or Normative Concept?"* Prepared for delivery at the meeting of Midwest Political Science Association, 1974, p. 17.

within this mode of classification is the relative stress various thinkers place on the value of individual liberty.

NEGATIVE FREEDOM AND INDIVIDUAL RIGHTS

At this extreme of our continuum, are those who put great emphasis on freedom, particularly for individuals. They believe that individual liberty is of such great importance that it should take precedence over collective interests. As they understand liberty it is the greatest possible opportunity to make as many choices as possible, a situation that requires the least possible exterior restrictions upon an individual. They believe that a collectivity cannot be given the authority to restrict important rights of the individual person. Their focus has been on what is usually called negative freedom. That is, they look at freedom as something that is threatened by environmental forces, most often by the state, and that must be protected at all times by vigilance. The term "negative freedom" invokes the idea that freedom must be preserved by negating the elements which are constantly seeking to diminish it. For them the battle for freedom is a negative battle in that it involves fighting off these forces. Thus they have always sought to erect barriers of "rights" around people's liberties to keep unwanted interferences at bay.

Negative freedom is the classic doctrine of the great liberal theorists beginning in the seventeenth century with Hobbes and Locke. They understood human beings in a framework that saw them as naturally free, as naturally able to make choices without much restriction. But they also did not think people were capable of getting on well with each other without some government, without some checks on unbridled liberty. Hence they believed that government was formed to check the few or the many that abused others in pursuit of their self-interest. The true aim of government was to realize as much liberty as possible and to protect as many rights as possible. Yet government was a danger and often had proven to be so. Liberty could be threatened and often was by governments who went beyond their minimum functions of providing order for liberty. The signers of the Declaration of Independence had just this concept of negative liberty. For them the British government had exceeded its task of providing a safe environment for the use of liberties. It had to be thrown off because it repeatedly transgressed against basic liberties that people had a natural right to exercise.

The term "right" is a very important one. A right is an absolute that cannot be denied by any person or authority. This absolute is the just and universal claim of all individuals that flows from their very personhood and not from any particular rank or status (although there are specific status-oriented rights that some theorists recognize). These absolute rights are held to exist in nature as natural rights. Certain privileges are part and parcel of being human—they are inexorably natural.

There are several categories of commonly asserted rights. One of these is the right of religious freedom. It is usually claimed to be a natural right and is often a protected legal right. As it is found in the U. S. Constitution (which is a fairly typical statement), this right guarantees freedom from religious persecution and freedom to practice whatever religion one believes. It guarantees the right to claim even that no God exists.

Religious freedom rights have a long history. People have long been persecuted, tortured, or killed in the name of religious absolutism and in places like Northern Ireland and the Middle East, religious hatred enters into the political controversies that divide people and governments today. Many liberal theorists conclude that the only way to avoid such religious disputes is to prevent any religious group or sect from gaining control of the state by guaranteeing freedom of worship to all theological persuasions, no matter how bizarre or unpopular as long as they are coincident with public safety. This pragmatic permission is important in itself; however, religious rights are extremely important to the liberal tradition because of a widespread belief that they reflect the pervasive religiosity of mankind and the sacrosanct nature of free religious expression.

Another, and related, category of rights that many often affirm may be called the rights of conscience. Although Henry Thoreau's and Martin Luther King's writings[4] are the examples most familiar to contemporary American students, Europeans like John Stuart Mill and Alexis de Tocqueville[5] were prominent advocates of this right as well. Proponents of a right to conscience assert that individuals should be allowed to follow the dictates of their own carefully considered ideas about morality and that no person or group, public or private, should interfere. Advocates of conscience rights agree that individuals must be allowed to follow their own consciences when faced with commands from a political community to fight in immoral wars or commit genocide or change their individual tastes and styles of living even if the vast majority of the citizenry objects. This raises the problem of tyranny of the majority that is so upsetting to many believers in rights to conscience. It makes no difference to them whether the source of an unjust command is a dictator acting alone or the pressure of tens of millions of neighbors and fellow citizens—if one is commanded to do evil, the result is tyranny. Leonard Hobhouse puts it in this manner:

---

[4]For a good survey of Thoreau's writings, see Milton Meltzer, Editor, *Thoreau: People, Principles and Politics* (New York: Hill and Wang, 1963).

[5]See Marshall Cohen, Editor, *The Philosophy of John Stuart Mill* (New York: Modern Library, 1961); Alexis, de Tocqueville, *Democracy in America* (New York: Schocken Books, 1961).

. . . liberty is no mere formula of law or the restriction of law. There may be a tyranny of custom, a tyranny of opinion, even a tyranny of circumstance, as real as any tyranny of government and more pervasive.[6]

John Stuart Mill was so insistent, in fact, that he claimed the right of individual freedom of conscience was absolute—no government or majority could restrict it at all, save only in the rare circumstances where its exercise would harm others. De Tocqueville warned about the dangers of a majoritarian tyranny that would erase individual liberties in early American society. Thoreau, too, was famous for the justification of his resistance against the laws that supported the slavery that he strongly opposed. He felt that it was a citizen's duty to employ his right of conscience by disobeying laws and governments that persisted in support of the immorality of slavery.

While this right has been invoked by some noble people in just causes, and while it always seems to have the aura of great moral authority about it, there are problems with it that cannot be glossed over lightly. The principal problem is the source of the right itself, the conscience. Some people describe conscience as the sum total of one's moral values derived from our respective socializations through relatives, schools, friends, churches, and so on. It is not, under this reading, anything more than an expression of one's environment and scarcely to be trusted as a statement of eternal or, indeed, any morality. Still others suspect that too often what is called conscience is merely a fancy name for one's more or less spontaneous whims, or that beneath its imposing traditional moral grandeur may frequently be found shrewd self-interest. Others, of course, believe that we have a moral sense or through reason and intuition access to a moral standard, represented in our conscience that quite transcends our environment, our whims, or our self-interest. This indeed was the whole point of Martin Luther King's campaigns for change through nonviolent action. The stubborn suffering involved was intended as a mechanism to awaken in all white people their conscience, to activate the truth all of us.

No matter which interpretation one agrees with, it is nonetheless fair to warn that the right to conscience must be investigated in every case with some carefulness. While it is reasonable to respect the rights of conscience and to be guided by conscience, we need to remember that some who pursue the rights of conscience are doing no more than attempting to imbue their belief with a mystical or sacrosanct aura that covers over what are strictly personal opinions. Moreover, those who appeal to conscience tend to assume that their conscience is automatically right, no matter what it tells us, as well as that one who invokes it has an absolute right to follow it no matter what the political implications might

---

[6]Leonard Hobhouse in Sidorsky, Editor, *The Liberal Tradition in European Thought* (New York: Capricorn, 1971), p. 99.

be. We do not agree that it is automatically sacred and it is our position that a right of conscience is valid not when its "truth" is proclaimed, but only when its source is probed and its dictates are conscientiously prescribed and argued as to their moral worth. It is quite irrational to invoke the right of conscience as the only rationale for a sweeping political position if that position is not justifiable by reasoned moral argumentation as well. For us, conscience is best looked on as a possible source of morality rather than the substance of it.

We must face the fact that consciences vary extensively. People on each side of most conflicts have claimed that their consciences compelled their actions. Perhaps they did, but simple assertions of rights based on conscience do not always make very convincing moral cases and certainly offer no acceptable proof. Advocates of rights to conscience like Thoreau often do not feel obligated to give adequate and detailed rationales for their positions of conscience that they have elevated to sanctity. They claim that their moral position is consistent with "the laws of nature," "right reason," or "divine revelation." People either see truth or they do not. Conscience advocates often claim that there is no need to explain or justify "the laws of nature" to those who cannot comprehend them because they are defective in reasoning ability. Such claims cannot be refuted because they do not rest on verifiable argumentation.

There are other problems with conscience especially if it is held to be an unlimited right. A mere whim or the result of temporarily clouded reasoning powers may be mistaken for conscience with great political consequences. Resistance and absolute denial of majorities are serious and often irreversible actions that should not be undertaken on a whim that might later be contradicted by a fully awakened conscience. Second, the absolute right of conscience has serious anarchic implications. If every individual is permitted to nullify the values and policies of the political community as his conscience dictates, there cannot be a political community. There are morally valid reasons for and situations when resistance should be undertaken (see Chapter 8 "Authority and Revolt") but advocates of an unlimited right to conscience go far beyond any theory of authority and revolt that recognizes the value of political communities.

Conversely, conscience must be respected as a stance when it is invoked to sustain the moral claims of individuals against statist or social values and demands that compel repugnant behavior. However, if rights are claimed for this reason they are subject to the same evaluation as any other claim of political morality. They have no automatic supremacy.

We should not reject rights of conscience out of hand, but we should be aware of the absolutist and the specious nature of the claims as they are frequently advanced. Mill is correct when he claims that people have private and public rights to pursue their own needs and desires as long as they do not directly hurt others by doing so, thereby claiming an importance for liberty that extends it up to the frontiers of basic equality. However, there is no substitute for a commitment to moral reasoning if we are to respect other people. This point is recognized by the activists who believe in conscience-informed civil disobedience. They make a careful effort to explain the reason for their actions and seek to convert others to their belief. This was the policy advocated by Martin Luther King, Jr. and it is the method practiced by many Quakers in the peace movement today.

Another alleged right, one of the most controversial, is the right to own and use private property. Property! The very word brings out some of the most intense passion and bitter arguments among human beings. There are many versions or degrees of this right, or liberty, to own property that different thinkers have defended over its long history. Some theorists have upheld the right to own property subject to a number of restrictions imposed by the general political community. Others have had a much more sweeping conception of property right, seeing it as virtually limitless. Certainly it has played an important part in Western political thought, especially since the rise of capitalism, and its most vigorous and sweeping advocates have been the so-called laissez-faire liberals.[7]

Although many theorists have set forth the concept of laissez-faire, the most readable and understandable is the eighteenth-century Briton John Locke.[8] Locke sought to secure the rights of a property owning class against both kings and commoners. In the present era, such thinkers as Milton Friedman, the University of Chicago economist and magazine columnist,[9] and William F. Buckley of television and newspaper fame remain sympathetic and seek to carry on much of the laissez-faire tradition. They have the enthusiastic support of many millions of Americans.

Laissez-faire, literal French for "to leave alone," is understood by its advocates to mean that property rights, the acquisition, use, and social implications of material goods, and the power of capital are inviolable and should not be tampered with by any alleged public interest. While its origins go back to the idea of social contract[10] advanced by the propertied against the claims of divine-right kings and have been used to secure property from restrictions, it reached its zenith with the rise of capitalism which resulted from the industrial revolution. Supporters of laissez-faire used the doctrine to justify their accumulation and exploitation of vast amounts of property not just in land but in factories and the fruits of production made possible by and necessary for the industrial revolution. Capitalists employed their property rights to achieve virtually absolute reign over the livelihood of millions of workers. It was used as a justification

---

[7]A good explanation and critique of this position is found in John M. Keynes, *The End of Laissez Faire*, in Sidorsky, op. cit.

[8]John Locke, "*Second Treatise on Government*," in Barker, Editor, *The Social Contract* (New York: Oxford University Press, 1962).

[9]He writes a column for *Newsweek Magazine*, Newsweek, Inc., New York.

[10]See Barker's introduction to his *Social Contract*, op. cit., for an excellent analysis of the idea of social contract theory.

for industrialists' opposition to child-labor regulation laws, wage and hour laws, and environmental controls of industry that would prevent the contamination of our natural resources, and it was made into a successful defense against critics of the social ills caused by the industrial revolution that allowed the "robber barons" of Europe and America to build great industrial and financial empires with the labor of ordinary citizens.

Though the use of a broad laissez-faire conception of the rights of property as a barrier against social regulation is still with us, it is gradually giving way to a grudging recognition that rights of property are not inviolate and that we must consider how others are affected by the uses of property. But today the danger of the concept of an absolute right to property remains the fact that it can permit private accumulations of power that rival and even surpass governmental authorities, as witness the power and resources of our present multinational corporations like International Telephone and Telegraph and Exxon to plot political revolutions or evade national regulation by moving headquarters and subsidiaries across borders.

There is also the problem of equality (see Chapter 6, "Justice"). It may be fair to give everyone an equal right to unrestricted acquisition and control of property if there is an unlimited amount of property and if all people are equally equipped to get and hold it. However, the industrial revolution was responsible for the permanent disappearance of those conditions if they ever did exist. People do not start out in life equally—they are differentially equipped with wealth, social advantages, family connections, accidents of birth like race, and many other differences. Thus, some start with a tremendous advantage in their ability to monopolize goods and power. As on a track used for running foot races, those who have the inside lane will win every time (assuming roughly equal running speeds) because that lane is shorter. "Justice," in modern track-and-field events, dictates that the starting point be staggered, insuring real and not alleged equality of opportunity to win the race. So it is with unrestricted property rights. They are unjust because the claimed liberty for all to have the rights of property does not exist in a stratified society with finite resources.

This does not mean that more limited property rights are ridiculous or automatically unjust. Instead, the laissez-faire position that was once valid against arbitrary kingly incursions on the interests of a nonroyal property class could not stand up when conditions changed from those of its original application. The question more often today becomes whether unrestricted property rights can supply what the utilitarians refer to as the greater good for the greatest number, an illusive but necessary balance of public needs with private interests. Most Western thinkers today do not ignore or dismiss the right of property altogether, but most do not think about it as an unrestricted right. Instead, they talk of property rights as one right among a number with which it will not always agree.

They visualize a complex balance of many rights, including property rights, with the general aim of trying to achieve the greatest good for a society as a whole. This objective necessarily involves restrictions on property rights and, for some thinkers, drastic limitations on such rights.

Another group of rights with which we are all familiar today are the rights to free speech, free press, and assembly. These basic political rights are, like the others, often derived from natural laws, but as often today are based on the utilitarian argument that they are essential to the achievement of a satisfactory form of human self-government. No rights are more familiar to the American tradition of politics and none have been more honored (in theory, and sometimes in practice) in American history. But even these rights are rarely held to be absolute in constitutional practice. There are limitations to what can be said (if a speech causes a riot), what can be printed (libel laws), and what kinds of meetings may be held (a meeting to plan treason) that few theorists of these basic rights ever dispute.

The First Amendment to the United States Constitution, which provides for these rights, is an almost classic case of the negative freedom philosophy in writing. For the First Amendment provides that "Congress shall make no law" to block these rights. The image it forms is one that suggests that rights are possessions that must be protected against government above all and that are in constant danger, a doctrine that liberals for centuries have held to be self-evident and inescapable.

A final group of rights that have been important to those who advocate negative freedom are a broad class of procedural privileges. These rights are the basic philosophical underpinnings of the "due process clause" of the U.S. Constitution and are widely recognized in most Western governmental and private organizations. This basis of the Western judicial system, with its roots deep in England's common law heritage, was intimately associated with the demands of property owners in preindustrial times that their property not be taken through taxation or otherwise without a series of fair hearings and appeals. It was, and continues to be, advanced by the accused and defenders of the unpopular who wish to protect themselves from arbitrary and/or bigoted actions by governmental officials. Champions of procedural rights ask that every person subject to criminal prosecution, job dismissal, and other circumstances of personal jeopardy be entitled to a fair and open hearing on the case. Included are rights to confront and question accusers, rights to expert counsel, rights to jury trials in criminal cases, and many other "due process" procedures.

The idea is that people deserve equal justice and that due process as a procedure will insure the substance of a just outcome. Every citizen is deemed to have the right to a fair hearing when in jeopardy because that is the only way proceduralists believe we can guarantee substantive outcomes of fairness. (See

Chapter 6, "Justice," for a detailed analysis of these values.) If procedures are so rigged that one side is automatically favored, a hearing is going to be a sham every time.

But the faith that some liberals have that procedural rights and lengthy and exhaustive procedures being secured for all will automatically result in just outcomes is naive.[11] Procedure is a necessary but not sufficient safeguard of individual and community interests. In addition to it, well-conceived and morally defensible definitions of crimes and punishments are necessary for justice. Even the best procedures followed in the service of poor, discriminatory, or arbitrary laws and regulations cannot guarantee fairness. Substance cannot be guaranteed by procedure alone because it is possible for a defendant to be the victim of prejudice by even the most carefully selected judge and jury if he is part of an unpopular minority and espouses a cause that is met with pervasive public hatred and hysteria. Thus, justice goes well beyond procedure and those advocates of procedural rights who have faith in an "invisible hand" of fair procedures ensuring automatically just outcomes must look to more reliable tenets of political morality if they are to be sure of justice being done.

This important point is all too often obscured by Western legalists and lawyers who make a virtual fetish out of due process rights. Those like the able legalist scholar Lon Fuller, who talk of the "inner morality" of law as if it were justice, direct us away from asking whether the broader political and social system in which procedural rights operate is itself just.[12] They wish to reduce justice to a matter of procedures instead of recognizing, as we do in our later chapter on justice, that due process rights are only one aspect of an entire social world that may or may not be just. For example, even if minority members of a society have their full due process rights in a trial, exclusive concentration on this fact may lead us away from asking whether the life situations of those minority members are such that the society in a broader sense treats them unjustly. Surely the latter is at least as important a question.

Problems With the Negative Liberty Approach

There are several difficulties with an approach to freedom that proceeds through negative liberty. First, one has to be clear where the source of liberty is. Very often arguments on this subject consist in little more than a claim for a liberty without an explanation regarding what the ultimate grounding of this liberty is. We have seen that in the Western tradition this source is very often natural rights, and, if this is the position, one that we are not unsympathetic to, there are further

---

[11]The wisdom of these procedures not withstanding, there are grave problems of implementing them universally, as the recent U.S. Supreme Court decisions in the Miranda case and others have shown.

[12]Lon Fuller, *The Morality of Law* (New Haven: Yale University Press, 1964).

matters that deserve attention. We have argued that merely asserting the existence of a natural right is of no particular help to anyone, nor is it especially convincing. One who claims a natural right must make some effort to explain how he or she has obtained knowledge of this natural truth. Contrary to Jefferson and the Declaration of Independence, rights are not self-evident or obvious, and they cannot be sustained by this method. A careful and conscientious effort must be made to demonstrate as best one can that such rights are basic to what it means to be human, are basic to what is natural for human beings. It often helps to demonstrate that one's conception of a right has been held by other thinkers of the past, not because this appeal to authority proves anything, but because it allays the reasonable fear that the claim of a natural right for this or that liberty, being difficult to disprove, may be used as a quick defense when all else fails.

Second, if one employs a natural right basis for liberty or anything else, it is important to be clear about just what that natural right encompasses. A right to liberty is no more than a vague abstraction that includes everything and thus nothing. Liberties are specific: the right to freedom of speech, the right to freedom of the press, and so on—not the right to "freedom." The curse of political theory is vagueness and grand abstractions that no one really means and that no one can really understand.

Third, excessive reliance on a natural rights basis for liberty often avoids the hard question of the relations between one kind or another of liberty and the social and political order at large. A natural rights basis for liberties often is an intensely individualistic approach, and its implications should, at the least, be pondered. For the natural-rights approach views liberties as the domain of each and every individual against all else and all others. It proclaims the individual as the supreme arbiter over all else. How far do we want to carry this doctrine? Moreover, we should ask ourselves about the social basis for rights. Whether or not we think that the basic liberties we favor are natural in their origin, it is a fact that political communities are the context in which they are fulfilled and, indeed, the context in which they are often denied. We cannot ignore our roles and lives in the broader social life of a political community by ceaselessly talking in terms of natural rights.

Finally, there is the root question, far beyond the question of the adequacy of a natural rights basis of most negative liberty arguments, of whether or not the Western tradition of thinking about liberty in terms of negative liberty is very useful. Modern analytic philosophers—those who think about our language in making political arguments—raise serious doubts on this issue. Perhaps the most exciting and most challenging attack on negative liberty as a way to understand the nature of freedom has come from the political philosopher Gerald MacCallum.[13] He argues that when political theorists in the Western tradition

---

[13]G. MacCallum, "Negative & Positive Freedom," The *Philosophical Review* LXXVI, 1967, pp. 312–334.

talk of liberty they speak too much as if it were a possession that exists only by the removal of another force that blocks its exercise. In other words, they talk of negative liberty.

In fact, MacCallum's analysis of ordinary language shows that, when we speak of freedom, what we really say is that we want to be "free from" (the language of those who are in the negative liberty tradition) in order to be "free to" do something. We never have in mind general abstractions like freedom conceived as the absence of all restraint, nor anything of the sort. Instead, we are interested in removing a specific blockage *in order to* accomplish, or have the opportunity to accomplish, a specific positive action. Liberty is not, as many who are sympathetic to negative liberty imagine, a possession that we want to hold inviolate forever, but an instrument that we want to use for specific purposes. By this understanding, this unpacking of the concept of liberty as the philosophers say, we should talk less of the natural right to liberty and more for instance, of the right to free speech undeterred by the government for the purpose of making our voices heard in the political system. And, indeed, MacCallum argues convincingly, this is exactly what we do in practice. The enormous advantage of his linguistic discovery is that it allows arguments in political theory to move from sweeping assertions about liberty in general to specific liberties, specific limitations, and specific purposes for which a liberty is to be exercised. On these matters meaningful arguments can be made, and liberty can return from the realm of vague rhetoric to the arena of concrete argument.

POSITIVE FREEDOM AND THE CONCEPT OF THE ORGANIC COMMUNITY

Political thinkers who believe in the concept of positive freedom are at the opposite pole of our continuum of positions of liberty. As negative freedom envisions a very small role for the state in the lives of citizens and concentrates on rights that protect individuals against collective claims, so positive freedom as an opposing approach envisions the political community playing an active role in the lives of citizens and puts a greater premium on collective privileges and interest than it does on individual rights. Included in this group are such classical giants like Plato[14] and Aristotle and modern thinkers as Hegel, Marx and Rousseau.[15]

These political theorists generally hold that human beings are not self-contained centers of consciousness and being. As biological organisms they

[14]See, for example, Plato, *The Republic,* A. Bloom, Editor (New York: Basic Books, 1968).
[15]A good brief discussion of Hegel and Marx as organicists can be found in B. J. Diggs, *The State, Justice and the Common Good* (Glenview, Ill.: Scott, Foresman, 1974), pp. 151–158. See Jean Jacques Rousseau, "The Social Contract" in Barker, Editor, *The Social Contract,* op. cit.

might be able to survive alone under favorable conditions but they only take on their "true" humanity as components or organs in a collectivity such as the Greek city-state, the General Will of Rousseau or the classless society that Marx hints at. In the organicist viewpoint, each person is an interdependent component of the whole community that, like a living organism, is a satisfying collectivity which is greater than the simple sum of each of the components.[16] The community is both the product and the ultimate definer of each of its members. As a natural organism it receives its "life" from the contributions of each part but it also gives meaningful life to each member. The citizens (organs) of the organism (political community) cannot live apart from each other any more than the heart can live a normal life outside of the human body and vice versa according to this biological analogy. Thus, the organic polity exists because of the interactions of each of its citizens, but every person in the polity is a real citizen instead of a solitary human animal because of his participation in a meaningful whole.

Organic theorists define liberty as a political value in a way that is quite different from the familiar Western, negative liberty perspective. To them, liberty is the result of participation in a political collectivity. Many of these theorists, especially Hegel and Plato, feel that genuine freedom is not the individual liberties that advocates of personal rights imagine because that leads to a solitary atomism that cuts people off from meaningful political interaction. Instead, genuine freedom is the increased opportunities and satisfactions that are the result of the civilized political life that only an organic community can supply. The options of virtue, comfort, and interpersonal relationships that allow all parties to prosper spiritually and materially are truly the liberation of the human potential—what frees people to be "genuinely human." Thus, while one who can do as he pleases is technically free, in reality he has no fellow citizens and mutual institutions to make liberty meaningful. It is a strange concept to Western individualistic ears but is advanced by these theorists without cynicism or ulterior motives.

There is also a strand of Western liberalism called positive freedom, which split off from the original laissez-faire advocates because of the inadequacy of laissez-faire prescriptions for the problems of complex industrial societies. These revisionist liberal theorists represented by the political theorist T. H. Green and many others have an implicit organicism in their belief that the state ought to intervene to stop the excesses of powerful individuals exercising their rights exploitatively. They feel the community is comprised of individuals who have a collective interest, often termed the public interest or the common good, which is the embodiment of the collectivity and exists in order to provide the greatest good for the greatest number or a similar goal. Thus, they feel that individuals are

---

[16]Diggs, op. cit., p. 152.

best served by a cordial and mutually supportive relationship with fellow citizens that depends on limiting excessive individualism.

PROBLEMS WITH THE ORGANIC OR POSITIVE FREEDOM IDEA OF LIBERTY

The organic or positive freedom idea of genuine liberty as collective participation rather than protection from others through individual rights is not wholly satisfactory. One reason is conceptual and takes us back to MacCallum's analysis of the linguistic nature of freedom. Just as MacCallum suggests that we do not really mean to speak of freedom in an exclusively negative framework, solely as freedom from restraints, we also do not mean to refer to it only as the right to do something, in this case as the right to collective fulfillment in society. It is on this side that those who stress positive freedom concentrate to the exclusion of freedom that involves choice and the absence of limitations on choice. Those who look fondly on positive freedom are surely right to acknowledge that viewing freedom as an abstract right that we somehow possess in lonely individuality is not what anyone really means by freedom, but they go far too far in the other direction and potentially swallow up freedom as choice in the "freedom to" participate in an organic society in which too often people have no choice.

There is also the problem of conceiving of a whole, in this case a political community, as being greater than its sum of its parts. It makes sense to stress that people must interact politically and that individual rights must be limited by social proximity requirements (as those sympathetic to positive freedom seem to want to do), but it is hard to imagine why a polity should exist for any other reason than to provide a better life for its individual members than they would have without it. Surely the interests of the collectivity add up to at least the sum of its parts and possibly even a bit beyond in order to control exploitative behavior. Nevertheless, it does not seem correct to carry that recognition the distance that advocates of an organic concept of liberty have. That runs the risk of putting the end of an alleged public interest on so high a pedestal that it will allow the devaluation of individuals. This is dangerous tendency in any theory that does not guarantee some basic individual protections through limitations on collective actions that may deny individualism.

Advocates of organic freedom often fail to consider each individual as important, regardless of his reciprocity to others that can enhance but not define his value as a human being and a citizen. In their stress on community interests they can go too far in destroying individual liberty. We may say that in reacting against the negative freedom perspective, they often go too far in the right direction.

Still, the organic theory of liberty does face the social and political dimensions of liberty squarely. It recognizes that the advocacy of isolated and egotistic personal liberty ignores the political dimension of the life of a citizen. It is quite right to point out to us that liberty that guarantees an extreme atomistic individualism leads not only to social chaos but to less real liberty to accomplish what one needs or enjoys. As a complete theory of liberty it leaves much to be desired, but as a series of valid insights and a corrective to negative freedom, it is worthy of consideration.

SOCIAL LIBERTY AND THE BALANCE OF RIGHTS

The final category in our typology reflects our view and that of those who see the defects of both negative and positive liberty. We call this the position of social liberty, because it recognizes individual rights modified by an appreciation of collective demands. It perceives problems with too much negative liberty but resists organic outlooks on liberty as well. Thomas Hobbes, for example, in his Leviathan[17] predicted that absolute liberty would lead to a "war of all against all" in a "state of nature" where life would be "solitary, poor, nasty, brutish and short." He argued that the strong would exploit the weak in the ceaseless competition for security in a world of finite resources and no person was so strong that he could afford to turn his back or sleep without fear of having a coalition of weaker people attack him and wrest away his gains. On the other hand, Hobbes saw that some liberty was valuable. In the same work he cautioned that all citizens must have absolute dominion over their own lives and bodies. Nobody could kill or torture them, even in pursuit of the all important public order that he prescribed as the antidote for too much freedom, because order existed for people and not vice versa. The authors of our American Constitution went even further. They eventually provided for negative liberties in the Bill of Rights in order to preserve individual integrity but wrote a constitution that distrusted popular wisdom and made it difficult for a majority of citizens to control the organs of government to translate individual liberties into policy supportive of public needs. They were afraid of a tyranny of the majority that, in their view, would be a passionate and undisciplined lowest common denominator like an emotional mob. In the same vein, Mill pointed out that lack of negative liberty would tend to allow those in power to become a permanent establishment that would stifle the human potential in all of us.

We agree without reluctance that some liberty (even much liberty, as Mill would have it) is necessary for individual citizens. However, we do not see why such a recognition must be extended to its absolute limits. We maintain that just

[17]Thomas Hobbes, Leviathan (New York: Collier, 1962).

as there are good reasons to have liberty, there are also good reasons why there must be some limitations on the rights of individuals. We are still individualists, but recognize the political dimensions of our individual lives and, consequently, we appreciate the rights of the collectivity that limit individual freedom. Along with Mill we argue that individuals may pursue any kind of private behavior as long as it stays truly private—as long as it does not affect others directly and negatively. The moment others are intimidated by behavior, it is public and subject to public regulation for the good of the collectivity. Thus, the actions of the nineteenth-century robber barons certainly would be subject to public regulation because their individual liberties intruded in a rude manner on the lives of others. The liberty of all individuals (equal members of a collectivity, not a metaphysical community) must be protected in practice as well as in principle, not just the liberty of a chosen few with social "clout." We wish to use the political community as a force to intervene in political situations to protect the liberties of all by curbing the liberties of those who advance them at the expense of others. We look to the modern state to accomplish this task by default because it is the only sector in society today that has enough force to stand up to a General Motors. Ideally, it is the only institution that can act in the interests of everybody without favor and, consequently, it may have the neutrality to make its role effective in the face of bribes, threats, and other tools of modern political influence peddling.

There are, to be sure, many varieties of thinkers who are well disposed to a conception of social liberty. They range from Hobbes who favored definitive intervention in virtually any political problem in the name of order to Keynes who favored action to cure material poverty.[18] The variety of rationales for political limitations on individualism in the name of public interest constitutes an exhaustive catalogue. Social liberals as diverse as Freud and Bentham agreed on the need for a balance of individual and collective rights in spite of very diverse perceptions of what constitutes a defensible public interest. Freud, for example, justified social intervention on the ground that human nature needs opportunities for harmless displacement of aggressions if civilization is going to avoid a Hobbesian war.[19] Bentham justified it because he thought it would secure the greatest good (the absence of pain and the presence of pleasure) for the greatest number in society—the theory of utilitarianism.[20] Defenders of a concept of social liberty today agree that it is the major rationale for the modern welfare state and our federal government's reason for entry into industrial regulation, environmental protection, national defense, job supply, and a host

---

[18]Keynes in Sidorsky, op. cit., p. 292.
[19]Sigmund Freud, *Civilization and its Discontents* (New York: W. W. Norton, 1962).
[20]Jeremy Bentham, *Principles of Morality, Utility and Legislation*, privately printed in 1780 in London and republished in many places.

of other tasks. It is often claimed, with some merit, that the reason for such interventionist devices as Amtrak (The National Railroad Passenger Corporation) in the United States has not been an American desire to embrace social liberty, but a grudging recognition of the necessity to accept it and to act in the face of repeated failure of laissez-faire clothed in private enterprise in many areas of our society.[21] Analytically, what unites theorists of social liberty is the rejection of the extreme claims of collective as well as individual rights and a common embracement of a balance of these claims in a concept of a public interest that will integrate them as it simultaneously prevents the excesses of either.

The objective is a balance between claims of individuals and groups that restrains the excesses associated with allowing complete individual freedom in a political framework. It prohibits the powerful from consolidating their hegemony through exploitation and it actually gives more usable freedom and better personal options by providing a greater opportunity to develop resources and skills in a sound environment. Under such a doctrine, everybody is subject to restraint of antisocial behavior yet suffers little restraint in many sectors of life. This involves a gamble that the concept of an identifiable public interest in the form of specified restraints on individuals will not make the whole so important that it allows individuals to be discounted.

PROBLEMS WITH SOCIAL LIBERTY

The major problem with the attempt to balance individual liberty and collective decisions that see liberty in a social context and can sometimes conceivably increase the opportunity requisite for the exercise of choice, is that the balance in principle does not necessarily assist us greatly when we must come to make concrete decisions about liberty in any specific situation. A good illustration of this dilemma came in a recent referendum on massage parlors in Madison, Wisconsin. Among those who argued on both sides of the question as to whether they should be allowed to operate were those who were decidedly in favor of the concept of social liberty. Some contended that massage parlors were an obvious area where there was so little public affect that individual negative liberties ought to be dominant, and massage parlors left free to operate as they wished. Others insisted that what was at stake was the very quality of a society, the

---

[21]For a good discussion of the pros and cons of the welfare state in the United States, see Dolbeare and Edelman, *American Politics* (Lexington, Mass.: D. C. Heath and Company, 1974), Second Edition, especially Chapter Eight.

context in which people grow up and live. To permit massage parlors was to reify negative liberty without any real interest in the broader social context.

Dilemmas such as this one bother some people inordinately because they believe that there is, somehow, somewhere, a magic formula that we can invoke to decide what liberty really is or what commitment to liberty would really dictate in this or that specific situation. Alas, this hope is an illusion, for there is no such formula. What we can do is understand several images of liberty, the conceptual and normative arguments for and against each; we can propose and argue for the best possible image of liberty, as we have. But in every concrete decision there will be no substitute for an ongoing process of discussion and argument about what liberty is and should be. This discussion can proceed far more easily when we have in mind how liberty is alternatively viewed, but in the end discussion and choice will have to go on—fortunately.

CONCLUSION

In the final analysis, none of these types of liberty has an absolute monopoly on truth. The laissez-faire position, advanced in order to protect citizens from arbitrary and ruthless treatment by the state or powerful private interests is a valid one when threats do occur as they have throughout human history. Tyranny from whatever source is an ever-present danger and must be dealt with if overall human political interests are to be preserved. However, opening up gates in the fence erected against public power to allow the state to protect against private power misuse often opens up a gap that cannot easily be closed again. The state has an interest of its own and its power cannot be invoked from the heavens and then sent back at will. The gates are not easily closed and advocates of strong positive freedom must be very cautious that the public power they sanction can be controlled. Also, organic freedom does not remove the dangers of tyrannies of the majority about which Mill and de Tocqueville warned. Something must be done to control them if we are not going to suffer the stifling conformity and loss of individuality that can gnaw away at the vitality of any political community.

Sir Isaiah Berlin writes:

> What is true of the confusion of the two [negative and positive] freedoms, . . . holds in even greater measure of the stretching of the word to include an amalgam of other desirable things—equality, justice . . . and the other ends that men seek for their own sakes. This confusion is not merely a theoretical error. Those who are obsessed by the truth that negative freedom is worth little without sufficient conditions for its active exercise, or without the satisfaction of other human aspirations, are liable to minimize its importance, to deny it the very title of freedom . . . to forget that without it human life, both social and individual, withers away.[22]

[22]Berlin, pp. lviii-lix.

We are left with the need for a reasonable balance between too much and too little individual freedom. We need to balance individual and collective interests by a theory of liberty that is moderate, one that succeeds in balancing freedom in principle with equal political access to it. The desirability of liberty as a reasoned value calls for restraint and points to some variation of the social liberal position as desirable. The great advantage of the social liberals is that they are cognizant that liberty should not be perceived in a vacuum: it is a social value with political implications beyond strict individualism.

SUGGESTIONS FOR SUPPLEMENTARY READING

General

Flathman, Richard E., *Concepts in Social and Political Philosophy* (New York: Macmillan, 1973).

Nisbet, Robert, *The Social Philosophers* (New York: Thomas Y. Crowell, 1973).

Sigmund, Paul E., *Natural Law in Political Thought* (Cambridge, Mass: Winthrop Publishers, 1971).

Liberty

Berlin, Isaiah, *Four Essays On Liberty* (London: Oxford University Press, 1969).

Fuller, Lon, *The Morality of Law* (New Haven: Yale University Press, 1964).

MacCallum, G., "Negative & Positive Freedom" in *The Philosophical Review* LXXVI, 1967, pp. 312–334.

Mill, John Stuart, *On Liberty* (New York: E. P. Dutton and Company, 1951).

Oppenheim, Felix, *Dimensions of Freedom* (New York: St. Martins Press, 1971).

Rousseau, Jean Jacques, *The Discourses* (especially the second one) (New York: St. Martins Press, 1964).

Sidorsky, David, Editor, *The Liberal Tradition in European Thought* (New York: Capricorn, 1970).

Spitz, David, *The Liberal Idea of Freedom* (Tucson, Ariz.: The University of Arizona Press, 1964).

Wertheimer, A., "Is Social Freedom an Empirical or Normative Concept?", Paper for meetings of Midwest Political Science Association, 1974.

Liberty and Equality—II

5

Today liberty faces a number of great threats that constitute new instruments in the age-old effort by the powerful to eliminate its exercise. Thought control is by no means something remote that Americans think only goes on in China; it is a reality that is entirely possible everywhere through technological and mass-marketing features of modern civilization. The mass media holds an enormous sway over us today, and who can say with confidence that its powers do not raise serious questions indeed about freedom despite all affirmations about the right to a free press?

Much has been made of late as well of the possibilities contained in psychiatry or even psychosurgery for dealing destructively with those who do not conform, at the expense of our ideals of freedom. Some thinkers, such as Thomas Szasz, believe that the greatest contemporary threat to liberty today in the United States lies in the abuses of psychiatry, the attempt to solve mental problems by, he thinks, making people conform and sometimes, indeed, locking them in institutions if they do not.

In addition to the threats posed by the powerful, public or private, the traditional source of alarm regarding preserving human choice, there is a second great enemy that many political theorists have often singled out as a major danger to liberty—and that is *equality*. There is scant doubt that equality has been one of the great concerns of political philosophers for the past several centuries, sometimes in social life, sometimes in economic affairs, sometimes in politics, sometimes in all three. It has been an aspiration of thinkers as disparate as Jefferson, Martin Luther King, Jr., and the great European socialists. It has been attacked from Plato to modern American conservatives.

But, as is so often true in political philosophy, there has been no agreement about just exactly what equality means, much less what its value, if any, is. We take it that equality is not to be confused with the idea of sameness. No one and nothing is equal in this sense of sameness; no two people are equally smart or equally strong, nor are two snowflakes the same. Equality in the sense of sameness is not a condition found in nature. Instead, equality is about the concept of equivalency, about X and Y being equivalent to each other without necessarily being the same. No two dancers are the same, but they can be equally good. No two boxers are the same, but they can be equally powerful punchers. No two citizens are the same but they can be equally valuable.

The central assumption of egalitarians has always been that while people are different, they are equal in being people, in sharing a single characteristic that is more important than their many variations. The central political problem, and area of dispute, among egalitarians has always been how much of life should be directed toward the fundamental fact, and value, of human equality. What is sought is rarely sameness so much as the functional equality implied in having an equal say in political decisions and the benefits offered by society. For example, the Civil Rights Act of 1964 in the United States mandates that places of public accommodation, businesses, and institutions that represent themselves as serving the public, must offer their services to all comers regardless of race, creed, religion, and so forth. The Act demands equal opportunity and treatment on a variety of levels. The concept of equal treatment before the law is another example. Those who subscribe to this expression of equality contend that the rules and regulations of society should apply equally to everybody in society. Thus, a rich, articulate powerful white Anglo-Saxon Protestant should receive the same treatment and adjudication of an offense he might be charged with as a poor, inarticulate black woman charged with the same crime. A third illustration of equality is contained in socialist arguments that all people ought to have equal incomes. People may have varying skills and talents but they are all equally people, say the socialists, and therefore ought to have an equal income in order to maintain and develop their lives.

The age-old argument about the worth and extent of equality can best be pursued by examining in detail some of the positions that political philosophers have developed regarding it, by exploring some of the images and ideals of equality that echo throughout political thought.

THE CONSERVATIVE VIEW

For a long time conservatives have argued that equality is not a value at all, not least because it is so flatly at odds with what we know of the natural facts of life. They point to the readily observable fact that individuals are not born equal in size, appearance, intelligence, talent, wit, and a host of other characteristics. Nor do people evolve during life toward greater natural equality. Conservatives suggest that people are so far from equality in all characteristics that only a foolish polity or social system does not accommodate to this reality.

Many thinkers in every era from Plato in classical Athens to the present have maintained that we should accord deference and heightened opportunity to those who are obviously superior by birth or achievement in order to achieve a stable and satisfactory political and social system. They argue that societies must be led by superior people if they are to gain excellence and not to suffer from the stupidity that results when the superior yield to the warped, albeit well meant, demands of the inferior. Thinkers like Plato and Burke had no urge to condemn those who were obviously inferior. To the contrary, they sought a political society that renounced any equality in part because they wanted to protect those not endowed with greatness and to put their destinies in the hands of the wisest in society. The inferior were not to be punished or belittled but, instead, paternalistically guided for their own good.

Those who exalt the fact of inequality do not agree on what aspects of the human person are the crucial ones. Some build their case on inequalities of intelligence and insight (as Plato did), others on wealth or aristocratic lineage and education (Burke), religious piety (the Puritans), military skill, technical and scientific understanding (in the view of many American technocrats), and so on down an endless list. Much depends on which human characteristics a thinker most admires, but they all agree that in what they consider the most important features of human capability there are massive differences that no nation may safely or honestly ignore. There is also disagreement on how rulers should be picked. How can the inferior recognize qualities of greatness in those they select to rule? Should there be automatic hereditary political succession processes or should each generation be examined for qualities of greatness? Orthodox monarchists and Plato would disagree here.

The conservative position that people are not equal in talent and therefore should not be treated equally in politics is not very convincing. No matter what indexes of comparison we settle on, to say that people are not equal is true enough. However, we do not think the inference for political equality drawn from that observation by many conservatives is warranted. It is a major logical jump to move from the fact of clear patterns of human inequality to an argument that people should not be treated equally in politics or elsewhere in society. This is a normative decision that cannot be made by dwelling on the undeniable facts of human inequality. The question becomes whether or not people are equal in the most important way of all, as people, as participants in the human race. And it becomes the question of whether, however equal or unequal they are as living people, they should be considered equal in moral worth and thus possessing an equal right to political participation or to a decent socioeconomic existence. These are matters that call for hard normative argument, not citation of the realities of inequality. Moreover, the demands made on citizens even in a highly participatory democracy do not require excellence, only the recognition of self-interest and the vision required to imagine the general consequences of actions for others. Citizens in a representative democracy only tell the leadership what they want and perceive. And no authority, human or not, superior or inferior, can determine what people need with anywhere near the accuracy of a system that allows people to speak for themselves. Participatory politics require more political sophistication on the part of citizens but it may well be that this sophistication can be acquired through experience and education by ordinary people if they are given enough reason to try to do so.

There is also a moral case to be made for political equality beyond the truth that we are all common participants in the human race. People who live in a polity have an equal stake in the quality of its institutions, policies, and provisions for the general welfare. The village idiot and the president of a large corporation are both equal in their need for national defense or environmental protection. Political theorists like Paine, Rousseau, and Camus believed that people should have an equal say in policy decisions and implementations. Paine felt that people should not suffer the indignities of colonial rule partly because it denied colonials an equal stake in their lives. He exhorted his fellow Americans to rebel by claiming that they had responsibilities to overthrow an unjust polity and to institute one that would allow for equality and liberty.[1] Rousseau is probably the most radical egalitarian in our literature. He made sweeping moral claims on behalf of participation, decision making, and the equal distribution of political power. He saw that men were so interdependent that it would be self-defeating folly to treat them differently. Camus agreed, and argued that people must regard themselves as a unity. Any injustice done to one individual, no matter how remote, is a direct attack on the intergrity of the solidarity of all human beings. In order to resist the enemies of life, people must regard all as their brothers and sisters for only a unified rebellion against what he termed absurdity could establish life as a meaningful value. Life is an equal possession and value of everyone.[2]

In short, critics of a conservative position on equality make two main points. First, we are all intelligent enough to play a valid political role and no one is so

[1]Thomas Paine, *Common Sense* (Garden City: Doubleday, 1964).
[2]Albert Camus, *The Rebel* (New York: Vintage Books, 1956).

much more intelligent or superior in any relevant way to entitle him to rule others without at least their revokable consent. Second, we all are equally human, are equal in our worth as people, and possess an equal stake in our political communities. The conservative position must be rejected because it does not substantiate its case for inherent human differences as a justified rationale for political inequality.

THE COLLECTIVE FOCUS: EQUALITY AS CITIZENSHIP

Others view the citizen from a perspective that leads them to a different and more positive assessment of the value of equality in a political community. These political theorists see the individual differences among citizens but contend that the differential qualities of individuals are not politically significant. The most restrictive position held by those who favor equality focuses on the human need for order. Thomas Hobbes is the spokesman for political theorists who define political equality and restrict it to order. He argued that human beings were equal in obeying the dictates of their self-interest and in pursuing personal greed. Their desire to acquire and possess created the necessity for order as a means of insuring security. They were also equal because each possessed just enough reason to be able to contract, to give up most of their liberties, in return for an equal stake in the political order under a ruler who had the power to enforce the social contract. Therefore, since people are equal in their natural desires and have an equal stake in maintaining peace, equality means the protection of human life through political order. Hobbes' formulation is simple and sweeping: no person can escape his stake in the polity and each must submit to the Leviathan (ruler) who shows no favoritism in keeping order. Each citizen who transgresses on another must be dealt with swiftly and short of capital punishment or torture with the full force of the state power.

Locke and others had a different view of equality as order. In his desire to protect the property rights of individuals, Locke's social contract provided an equal right for each individual to protect his property, and, if a government was established, each property owner had an equal stake in securing his property privileges. Augustine had yet another view. He felt that all human beings in earthly societies were depraved and sinful and that they must all submit to the stern power of a king who ruled by divine right as vice-regent of the Lord in protecting citizens from themselves. Equality was harsh but it allowed men who were equally sinful to persevere in the "City of Man" while on their way to the "City of God" where such stern measures were not necessary since all who were permitted to enter had been purged of their sinful natures.

Under this concept, to be treated equally is to receive like treatment with other individuals in the same circumstances. It does not convey the meaning of any particular quality of treatment. Thus, in evaluating this or any other theory of equality, we must not confuse the word "equal" with something necessarily virtuous. We must look at the quality of the equality.

Those who view equality as residing in political order are on the right track but they have not traveled a sufficient distance on it. Theirs is a concept that is as yet too restricted. To be sure, order can only be conceived of as applicable to all or it would not be orderly, but we must ask whether it is worth the price Hobbes and others are willing to pay for it and inquire about what other values this concept ignores. To secure order Hobbes is willing to sacrifice much liberty as well as rights of ongoing political participation in order to secure what could become the equality of a prison. To be sure, Hobbes hoped that complete order under a sovereign would allow most people considerable choice, even considerable laissez-faire, in their daily lives, but his pessimistic view of human nature, seeing man as evil enough to destroy himself in a war of all against all if he is not restrained, made him very cautious. The trouble with those whose main emphasis is on order is their image of human nature/behavior. It is a pessimistic misreading of human behavior if we are to believe modern behavioral psychologists and anthropologists who say that human behavior is not so easily predictable and is capable of much greater variance than Hobbesians admit.

Human beings need more than order or equality of property rights to make the most of their potential in a polity. Order is only a means to goals like social justice, political legitimacy, balanced liberty and equality, and responsive political communities. We ought to be more interested in asking what kind of order are we looking for—what values will it secure and protect—rather than making unsupportable claims that equality ought to be concerned with peace at any price. We need peace, but if we are going to have to pay too much for it, we are only gaining a Pyrrhic victory. If we have to enslave ourselves to get to heaven or live in a prison to avoid death, we cannot wonder whether this kind of equality is worth the sacrifice.

SOCIAL AND ECONOMIC EQUALITY

The socialist tradition of equality which grew to maturity in the nineteenth century and is vigorously alive today, presents quite a contrasting image of what equality is all about. According to it the reality of common humanity requires that all people obtain equal fulfillment of their basic social and economic needs. For many socialists this requires state ownership of the means of production, and for all of them it requires at the least active governmental planning and a welfare state. They reason that political communities necessarily exist for the mutual satisfaction of human needs and that it does not make sense to allow access to great resources to some and to deny the benefits to all. If property is not held in common or if it is distributed unequally, some people garner more than their just share of the limited resources. They squander and waste the greater part of it while exploiting others by "stealing" their labor for ridiculously low wages or property shares. The result is a minority group of superrich whose monopoly of resources leaves the majority in relative poverty without access to what they need to survive let alone flourish.

Socialists are angered by this monopoly. They make a strong case for equal property rights for citizens and condemn property accumulations that go beyond reasonable needs. The only property that they feel should not be subject to common ownership (thus giving each an equal and just share under the auspices of the community) or regulation would be that what is needed for strictly personal use and that could not be used to exploit others.[3]

While the theory that equality should mean socioeconomic equality is attractive, it is flawed whenever it slips into too great evaluation of the material dimension of life. As we argue in Chapter 6, "Justice," concern for substantive equality in material goods is an important value, but there are many other needs and aspirations in life than the exclusively material one that motivates some socialists. Nor should we slip into the view that property relations are the sole important aspect of existence that somehow explains all things and that by a kind of "invisible hand" process analogous to that employed by classical economists will ensure that all will go smoothly in human existence once equal property rights or common ownership of the major means of production occur.

Many Marxists have a tendency to fall under these illusions, but Marx himself was more careful, particularly in his classic discussion in *The Critique of the Gotha Program*. There he made clear, as he had elsewhere, not only that human needs are various and complex, but also that formal equality in regard to property was far less an ideal than "each according to his needs," a rather different notion which we will explore in our justice chapter.[4]

EQUALITY AS SELF-GOVERNMENT

A number of democratic theorists suggest that equality is best understood as the equal power of all citizens to be sovereign, to be able to rule themselves. Theorists like Locke, Mill, Rousseau, and Jefferson claim that the rights of self-government for all people constitute an adequate definition of equality because governments make or influence virtually all of the politically significant

---

[3]See George Lichtheim, *The Origins of Socialism* (New York: Praeger, 1962).
[4]Karl Marx, *The Critique of the Gotha Program*, many sources.

decisions in a society and that equal access to decision-making status gives the citizens all the power they need to enjoy a good public life. As we saw in our chapter on democracy, democracy is a complex topic and we will not review its many aspects here. In this context, we are examining the ideas of those who argue that democracy secures all the equality we need in a political community.

Champions of the familiar Western concept of majority rule hold that true equality resides in allowing a majority to rule by enforcing its preferences (limited by individual rights to political dissent) on all who live in a polity. Equality is served by allowing each person to voice his opinion through the full exercise of his civil liberties and political participation, thereby having as much influence in policy decisions as anybody. They contend that no one should be allowed any more than his equal share of influence or voice because no one can speak for anyone else and each person is of great moral worth on his or her own. The only criterion for enfranchisement is to be a "two-legged being who walks upright and does not have feathers," to paraphrase Aristotle's semifacetious image of a human being.

Many majoritarian democrats are representative democrats who feel that popularly elected legislatures are the best mechanisms to represent majority views. Locke and Mill assert that the equality that citizens need is secured by guaranteeing a broad procedural right that will allow fair play and the right to try to become a part of a majority.

Majoritarian democracy's claim to equality is suspect because it affords genuinely equal treatment only to those who are on the winning side. If one happens to be on the defeated side—especially if one loses consistently—the equal opportunity to vote for representatives or policies begins to ring hollow even if people have an equal, if theoretical, chance to become part of a majority if they will only work as hard as the winners. Consistent losers might have this chance in situations where there is an almost equal split between partisans and the swaying of a few minds could change tne outcome or in situations where there was no automatic favoritism shown to proponents of a case regardless of its merits. The existence of genuinely pluralistic political communities that would give all people equal chance at majority status is a rare phenomenon. Virtually every polity has within its ranks groups of consistent losers in policy matters. Real political equality requires an equal ability to mobilize majorities and that is the deficiency in most political systems which espouse majoritarianism. Thus, it is difficult to agree with the theory of equality as majority rule when it does not take into account that it is almost impossible to equalize political weight and that the notion one-man, one-vote, of participatory rights, does not eliminate the structurally favored nor the slighted in the polity.

This concept of equality fails to confront the problem of the tyranny of the majority, the powerful and oppressive force of public opinion and the intolerance of differences that forces itself on minorities. It afflicts even those who have the resources to try to convert others to their case but who cannot get a fair hearing because their appeal falls on deafened ears. Sometimes these minorities are "cranks" but, in all-too-many instances, they are people who have a heightened moral sense and the courage to speak out against the injustices that most people would rather not be reminded about. The conscientious resistors to the U. S. war policies in Vietnam who spoke out throughout the 1960s are a poignant example. These minorities were not served equally by a majoritarian theory of equality.

Some other participatory democrats, including many among the New Left of the 1960s have suggested that the defects of majority democracy will be overcome when universal and direct participation actually takes place, participation that will negate the effects of legislative tyranny over the populace whether it originates by design or accident. They reason that if all people govern directly the problems of majority tyranny and consistent losers will disappear at the hands of a spirit of community.

Rousseau knew better, however. Through his concept of a general will, which will not allow a community to act unless all share a single voice on an issue, he realized that equality as universal access to political participation by itself is not a panacea and will not cure the problems of majoritarianism by an "invisible hand" theory of community. Community and a "general will" must be sought, nurtured, and waited for. They will not appear magically as a constant companion of participatory democracy. The hopes of the late New Left did not take such subtleties into account. Full citizen participation, if achievable, would still only be a procedural improvement over representative participation and it would not negate the potential for the tyranny of the majority in any polity. While majority tyranny is preferable to minority tyranny from the standpoint of the number of those oppressed, the usual participatory system is still majoritarian and still subject to the problems associated with most democratic theories. Problems cannot be defined out of existence with vague references to community and no machinery to implement them. Rousseau's "general will" might be impractical, but at least it is an attempt to substitute something—consensus—as a replacement for majoritarianism. A solution of the problems of representative democratic theories based on participation rights does not eliminate the reality that there are winners and losers on any policy question where consensus is absent. Participatory democracy only accomplishes the task of allowing the losers to speak for themselves instead of through imperfect representatives. This might slightly increase their access to potential majority formation, but it cannot make an unpopular minority more palatable to a majority conditioned to reject what they say. Consensus is remedial but it pays the heavy price of deadlock and inaction in the face of pressing problems or it must allow those who oppose the right to refuse to obey the law or policy in question. This raises the disturbing possibiility of the erosion of community mindedness.

For these reasons—and also because the theory does not fully extricate itself from charges that universal rights of participation could not be effective due to differences in articulateness, education, and social class, as well as the unpopularity of affilation—we must reject participatory democracy as the full measure of a definition of equality from a political perspective. Self-government is a commendable political theory and a valuable component of equality. Its pervasive rights of access to political decision processes make it broader than order, property rights, or any other theory of political equality we have examined, but it, too, does not go quite far enough.

A LAST POSITION

In the final analysis, we need a general doctrine of equality understood as basic human fairness. Indeed, all of what we have examined so far can come under a general doctrine of what many political theorists, most prominantly of late the philosopher John Rawls, refer to as fairness, the idea of being fair to all persons by treating them equally in light of the ways that they and their circumstances warrant.[5] Implicit in such a doctrine would be a value of life that respects all human beings and assumes that each deserves to be treated with equal dignity.

This basic idea of equality defined as fairness to all people is a concept that has surfaced often in the literature of political theory. Many thinkers agree that equality as fairness cannot embrace any rigid formulas of treating all in exactly the same way because people's needs and circumstances differ radically. An example is the progressive income tax laws found in most industrialized nations. They contain the idea that a rich individual can afford to pay a higher percentage of his income in taxes and still live comfortably than a poor person who would be left at the brink of starvation if he had to pay high tax rates. A 5 percent sales tax on food to a person on a minimum wage means much more than a 5 percent tax on a luxury automobile to a millionaire; the same tax rate does not have a fair or equal impact on the two of them. Thus, fairness dictates that the functional equivalent of equal treatment that might not be literally equal should be applied to people of different circumstances in a polity so that each would receive an equal amount of what is really required: fairness and respect for human dignity.

This theory has many attractions. First of all, it is broadly based. It focuses on a broad class of needs and situations that could conceivably encompass most of the problems needing equalization in a complex modern political community. It does not restrict itself to any rigid formulas that would limit its practical effec-

[5]John Rawls, *"Justice as Fairness"* in De Crespigny and Wertheimer, Contemporary Political Theory (New York: Atherton Press, 1970).

tiveness or its moral content. Its major flaw is that it is so vague that it can be defined in virtually any way without stretching it out of proportion. It is so elastic when applied to equality that it has no obviously discernible form.

In order to embrace the strengths of equality as fairness while avoiding its vagueness, we must tighten it and focus it on the specific problems of political communities. The specifics of a good equality theory ought to change as they are applied to different societies, but the valid moral principles behind specific prescriptions remain, regardless of given applications. A reformulation of fairness as the need for treating obvious equals equally and unequals unequally within a framework of equal opportunity will accomplish our goal. As we have seen, people are generally the same in their politically relevant characteristics and each citizen's claim to participation. They have the same political stake in a polity that consists of moral equals interacting with each other through common institutions and culture. Thus all citizens ought to have an equal political input into their political system, ought to expect equal enforcement of the laws, and should receive equal justice in the courts. As we shall argue in Chapter 6, "Justice," people are also equal, if not the same, in their basic economic needs and their society ought to guarantee them the realization of this equality.

In many other areas of life, however, people are scarcely equal. They are not equally good students, adept baseball players, skilled medical doctors, or competent mechanics. Here the essence of fairness, and thus equality, is to treat them as unequal and allow those who are especially talented to pursue the right to be superior, to be unequal. But we argue that this is only fair when people who are unequal in various characteristics start out with equal opportunity. Society should provide for an equalizing factor that puts all people on a starting block that has the same length of track in front of it, recalling our analogy to a footrace run on an oval track. Thus, people who are victims of racial, religious, sexual, or any other discrimination are given increased training and/or privileges of access to economic, political, or other kinds of opportunities (the equalizing of the track) in order to erase past inequalities—to equalize the running distance, so to speak.

This norm of equalization of opportunity takes on characteristic prescriptive forms in contemporary Western applications. It stresses economic opportunity through such devices as minority training and hiring programs (such as the ones the American automobile industry adopted after the Detroit riots demonstrated the discrimination built into their personnel policies), affirmative action programs, which demand that employers and the like seek minority persons in order to equalize personnel, students, or whatever is being counted, Job Corps Centers, which give vocational training to the victims of inadequate schools, equal rights statutes and other devices, which seek to reverse discrimination patterns of centuries.

Educational opportunity is another area of concern to an equalization of opportunity approach. People cannot succeed in a complex society unless they have the quality preparation that allows the poorly prepared to "catch up" and have an equal chance at educational benefits, from jobs to social consciousness. Thus, programs are needed here, too. Similarly, political opportunities like voter registration aid, equal apportionment, and civil liberties protection helps those who have been effectively drummed out of the polity by providing them with a citizen's rightful political efficacy.

These purposes may sound pleasant and worthwhile, but it would be a grievous mistake not to understand that they are, in fact, extremely difficult to achieve. The way is hazardous and by no means certain. The unpleasant truth is that many government programs to open up opportunity have not worked and the problems have often resulted from much more than too little money. People cannot be easily trained, jobs are not always available, and attitudes die hard. Above all, efforts to achieve greater political and economic equality as well as general opportunity face the redoubtable force of those who are simply not interested in surrendering what they have in order to accomplish this objective.

At a more principled level, many people fear that equality as fairness and equality of opportunity will result in a kind of leveling down in society. The reality is, however, that part of the aspiration of equality as fairness is to allow obvious unequals to reach their proper level. People who have a really equal opportunity at something and who are superior at it will excel. Furthermore, such excellence will be the result of genuine merit, not the result of unfair competition that gives winners an unjust advantage and losers a legitimate complaint. Soundly conceived, equality as fairness is freedom from prejudice, favoritism or official fraud, a theory of equality that could ensure citizens the fairness that is what human beings in a polity deserve and why political communities are justified.

This approach is the best that we can do in defining and applying the norm of political equality because it covers a sufficient range of human concerns to blanket virtually all of life with a desirable application of that value. Therefore, we conclude that equality as defined here is an invaluable component of any political theory. It is necessary but not sufficient to allow a good life to flourish in a complex political community. While it is not the definitive answer to all of our problems, it is powerful enough to command our sympathetic consideration.

LIBERTY AND EQUALITY

Now that we have explored some theories of liberty and equality in some depth, we return to an earlier theme: the interrelationship of liberty and equality. Everybody desires some kind of freedom and each of us wants to be considered as good as anybody else. But we cannot have everything. These desirable values tend to conflict in their interactions within a polity. We simply cannot have a broad spectrum of liberties as well as simultaneous equality in everything. Our alternatives thus are limited—we have to make choices between values.

For instance, we cannot have unlimited liberty of property rights and do much about providing equal opportunity for people in economic life. Nor can we provide people with a basically equal and decent environment without interfering with common attitudes that allow both individuals and businesses to do what they wish with their property. Similarly, how can we exalt the rights of conscience to untouchable heights and yet expect that we can have a democracy of equal citizens all subject to law? Nor can we doubt that the existence of a democracy that provides equal citizen participation may well lead to the passage of many laws that may restrict individual liberty.

But instead of lamenting that equality and liberty will often be in conflict, an unavoidable reality, we must consider what can be done about this problem. There are only three alternatives open to us that have any promise of desirable results. We could concentrate on liberty alone, on equality alone, or we could try to balance them to acquire the maximum advantages of each. The option of sticking with liberty and abandoning equality is not a very fruitful one. Without guarantees of equal treatment and rights for people who do not have greater natural abilities or favorable backgrounds, and without unlimited resources and a constantly expanding frontier available to all comers, the potential for violent or debilitating social conflict over resources and status is too great. Such conflict cannot help but stifle human development because it would siphon off too much effort of individuals and communities alike into mechanisms for competition and coping with its effects and leave precious little human energy or motivation that can be directed toward political accommodation and common betterment. An uneasy state of conflict and a constant race for position and security are more hallmarks of a state of war, albeit a cold one, than they are of a smoothly functioning political system that puts emphasis on mutual accommodation. To be free is fine as long as freedom is adapted to the needs of the political communities that citizens must have to reach their most desirable quality of existence. Unfortunately, liberty without equality will not supply that kind of adaptation by itself. Efforts to ameliorate the problems of liberty alone are reflected in theories of social freedom that go a long way toward supplying that kind of social framework precisely because they are not pure theories of freedom but, instead, incorporate the valuable restraints that equality can put on liberty.

Similarly, equality alone in any pure sense does not fare well as a morally acceptable option either. Equality often operates to limit freedom. If given *unlimited* rein, the requirement that people must have the same chances, rights, resources, skills, rewards, and status could prevent the flowering of any individual differences and talents and, with that, prevent the independent thought and spontaneity that prevents human life from being a static monotony devoid of any innovation and social change. Liberty is too precious to abandon. We must carefully justify any interference with it, whether in the name of equality, justice, order, authority, or what have you.[6] By the same token, we must and can justify limits on equality, as in the theory of social liberty or equality of opportunity. Vague concepts of a public interest will not do in this regard. The need must be clear and present and the remedy appropriate and limited enough so that it will not destroy the need served by liberty. Human beings need to be free as well as equal and liberty cannot be reduced too far lest human development be lost sight of and regimented dehumanization raise its specter. Equality alone can be just as pernicious a form of degradation as unrestricted liberty. We need to have ample amounts of it to modify the extremes of liberty and to guarantee that liberties are available to all, but any more than that can become a remedy worse than the disease.

Therefore, with the rejection of pure liberty or equality as viable options, our alternatives are reduced to this: some form of balance and coexistence between liberty and equality within a political community. A politically motivated and adapted balance between these values is the only way to secure the maximum possible benefits of both. Their operation in concert has the desirable effect of blunting the liabilities of each one as separate entities. Like vintage blended whiskies or pipe tobaccos, they can mellow each other and produce a smooth mixture of greater characteristics than each ingredient without its individual "bite."

Such a blend of the two values can be accomplished through the auspices of several kinds of political institutions. It is not the exclusive province of democracies and has been accomplished at times in virtually every type of polity. However, democracies with strong citizen participation in decision making have the most reliable likelihood of reaching and maintaining such a balance because they tend to tap the natural pluralism (not merely pay lip service to a pluralism preverted by imperfect democratic institutions) of large, reasonably free populations that have guarantees of equal opportunity and that will keep monopolistic establishments from forming and stifling diversity.

It is important to note, however, that a balance must be secured with the political interests and needs of the citizens firmly in view. Any pseudo-balance that is in the interests of a ruling class and merely co-opts citizens is fraudulent in conception as well as operation and will not accomplish what it ought to do.

These values do not have to be in a state of perfect balance in order to fulfill their moral functions. Values are not pieces of gold on a jeweler's scale that is constant and merely detects differences of weight. Societies are constantly

---

[6]See Richard Flathman's remarks on this in his *Concepts in Social and Political Philosophy* (New York: Macmillan, 1973), p. 264.

changing and so are their ideas of the best values. A valid balance between liberty and equality must have both values present in significant quantities but it can and sometimes should put more weight on the side of one or the other. A morally acceptable set of political values and prescriptions should be subjected to and the result of a lively political process resulting from the contributions of all citizens. It must adapt itself to the ever-changing needs of people that result from shifts in their environment as past policies and institutions combine in a kaleidoscope of social interactions. As conditions change there is a need for different values and political prescriptions to be emphasized. Yesterday's prescriptions may be obsolete tomorrow and the day after they may be valid once again. What is required above all else is the constant attention and perception of political theorists and policy makers so that the many possible combinations of these values may be culled for the most appropriate ones in any given political situation.

We think that the appropriate balance for the United States and the Western world at present should be composed of four aspects. First, we would continue to encourage the movement of recent years that has abolished some of the legal barriers to the free pursuit of individualism in such areas as dress, sexual behavior, and living arrangements. Here is realm of individual freedom that seems to us to be vital for the development and growth of each individual person. This would include a steady maintenance of basic political liberty to make one's voice heard.

At the same time, we must face the fact that the Western world, indeed the entire world, faces an inexorable crisis brought on by our unending interest in economic development and the consequent pollution and destruction of the environment. In this area it would seem that the realm of human choice will have to be curtailed and quite possibly drastically. As Robert Heilbroner points out, in his grim book, *The Human Prospect,* this will involve not just a restriction of private economic liberty of business but also a limitation on individual desires for endless and expanding consumer freedom.[7] Our concern for equality, not just an equally decent environment, but indeed an equal survival, requires attention to this equality at the sacrifice of this dimension of liberty, the liberty that is literally threatening to kill us.

Third, in order to achieve the equality of opportunity to participate politically and to have a chance to succeed in what we seek to do in life, to have a chance to make choices, we will have to undertake action that will undoubtedly require further restrictions of economic liberty and the liberty of property rights, subjects we discuss further in Chapter 6, "Justice." We know the truth is that we cannot have pure liberty and equality together and, in this case, as in others, it will be necessary to restrict property rights in order to maximize political equality and the liberty to develop for all people.

[7]Robert Heilbroner, *The Human Prospect* (New York: Norton, 1974).

But neither pursuit of individual liberty wherever possible nor the restriction of liberty in the name of survival, opportunity, and equality through the use of the state will ensure progress toward the highest aspiration we seek in the balance of liberty and equality, the furtherance of authentic individuals united in an awareness of common humanity. Our theory of authenticity holds that people need and ought to have arenas of both solidarity and spontaneity in social and political life. No institutions or programs or perfect balances of values can reach this point.[8]

We distinguish, from the first, simple equality from solidarity, for people can be equal in all respects before the law as well as before each other and at the same time remain strangers. They can have no way to relate to one another across the barriers of mistrust bred from the impersonal nature of a society that isolates each in a cocoon of relationships to institutes and aggregates instead of familiar personalities.

The particular balance of equality and liberty prescribed by this kind of approach is a mixture between solidarity and individual freedom. If citizens are secure in the knowledge that their needs will be satisfied with reasonable effort on their parts through an economic and political equality that recognizes individual variation and yet know that they will have great liberty for political, intellectual, and personal choice and individuality then perhaps they will someday have nothing to fear from others. There might not be the terrible compulsion toward conformity and majority tyranny that currently is an understandable defense mechanism adopted by people who half consciously resist being submerged in a whirlpool of lost identity through mass bureaucracy while surrendering to the fear of being different. The provision of the necessary and equal security for authentic individualism in conjunction with equality that does not operate through remote institutions and employs considerable participation of citizens in political structures is the great objective.

If diverse people can relate to "real" people and not to faceless statutes and regulations through countless bureaus full of recorded announcements and triplicate forms, then they have nothing to fear by being individuals. Liberty would be back in style as long as it did not extend to the point of depriving others of their needed equality or human survival. Perhaps people, no longer fearing each other, might come to like, enjoy, and respect each other—and human solidarity might grow. Equality and freedom could grow in a polity operating on a humanly proportioned plane, not one designed for the convenience of data processing machines and adapters of mass production technology to political situations.

A balance between liberty and equality of this nature is obviously utopian, but

---

[8]See Michael Weinstein's chapter on *"Socialism and Humanism"* in J. Orenstein and Louis Patsouras, Editors, *The Politics of Community* (Dubuque, Iowa: Kendall/Hunt, 1973). Marshall Berman, in his *The Politics of Authenticity* (New York: Atheneum, 1970), gave it a convenient name.

not at all a final panacea. First of all, like even the most successful prescriptions of political theory, it would merely be a temporary adaptation of some basic principles to a set of circumstances that will change. The forms it might take are impossible to suggest neatly, because the relations would be ever in flux and because this ideal has more to do with the spirit of human interaction than the laws and forms of government that might assist its realization. Second, like all political theories, there are no guarantees that it would work as well as its proponents claim. Still, even if it is not a panacea it is a suggestive theory of what the correct balance of liberty and equality ought to be in the postindustrial world.

CONCLUSION

The issues of liberty and equality thus converge in a theory that balances them through norms of considerable economic and political liberty, equal opportunity, and social liberty taken together. Liberty and equality cannot stand alone because there are no such things—only specific liberties and equalities in one or another area of life—and because they often conflict with each other. Nor can we look at equality and liberty in a framework that ignores other root political values such as democracy, justice, and political obligation. We cannot somehow escape the terrible complexities of trying to balance multiple values into a simple world such as the one Rousseau described as the beginning of the human experience. No doubt we would not want to do so either because that would mean abandoning the fruits of our development along with its liabilities. Instead, we agree with Rousseau that we must develop the functional equivalent of simple nobility by adapting it to the problems and demands of our age. We need to strike the right balance among our values to find a political community that allows individualism and community to flourish. There is no other way for modern individuals that will allow the maximum possible human development and provide the fruits of meaningful private lives in a noncoercive, responsive public sphere. There is no other way to experience the politics of accommodation, if not respect, in a postindustrial era. There is no other way to avoid the grave risks of destructive conflict. In the final analysis, we have nothing more than our values and moral vision to fall back on. There is every evidence that these will serve us amply if we will only use them.

SUGGESTIONS FOR SUPPLEMENTARY READINGS

Burke, Edmund, *An Appeal from the New to the Old Whigs* (Indianapolis: Library of Liberal Arts, 1962).
Gans, Herbert, *More Equality* (New York: Pantheon, 1973).

Heilbroner, Robert, *The Human Prospect* (New York: Norton, 1974).
Hobbes, Thomas, *Leviathan,* many publications.
Lichtheim, George, *The Origins of Socialism* (New York: Praeger, 1969).
Orenstein, Jeffrey and Louis Patsouras, Editors, *The Politics of Community* (Dubuque: Kendall/Hunt, 1973).
Plato, *The Republic,* many publications.
Rousseau, Jean Jacques, *The Social Contract,* many publications.

Justice

Everybody talks about justice every day and in many ways. We discuss justice when hearing of jury decisions and judicial sentences; we have opinions about the justness of our society and of our pay; we comment on the justice of professors' grades and the Academy Awards; we even call wars just or unjust. We employ ideas of individual justice and social justice, procedural and substantive justice, political and economic justice, even divine versus earthly justice.

We tend to speak so much about justice because we all assume that justice is a good thing and injustice a bad thing. Everybody wants a just society, just treatment in the courts, a just salary, and everyone is quick to denounce injustices. The trouble is, however, that few people seem to agree on exactly what justice is. Some think former Vice President Agnew got justice, others deny it; some say Lt. Calley was treated unjustly in receiving a ten-year sentence for the My Lai massacre while others insist he got full justice. It is the same with the Watergate defendants. Day after day people dispute whether justice is served in ordinary criminal cases of murder, rape, or drug dealing. They argue as well over the justice of decisions by public regulatory agencies to grant new rate formulas to airlines or the local gas and electric company. We may even con-

tend over justice with the policeman who hands us the speeding ticket or the Internal Revenue agent who challenges our tax returns. Justice is clearly a major issue that deserves our attention because we talk and disagree about it so often.

This chapter examines the nature of justice, making clear what some of the contending versions of justice are and suggesting a possible resolution to the disputes over justice. This will not be easy because justice is such a complicated and challenging concept. We use the word often enough and we have an intuitive sense of its proper meaning in one situation or another, but it is quite another task to formulate a clear notion of justice.

THE NATURE OF JUSTICE

If we can say that there is a just law, a just welfare policy, a just war or a just society, then it is obvious that justice covers a great deal of ground. Clearly it is a rich concept, capable of multiple uses with a variety of meaning and inferences. Yet we should understand from the beginning that the extraordinary richness of the concept should not lead us to confuse it with all of our moral judgments in or out of politics. Justice is by no means the only moral value, since it is obviously different from other moral values such as love or human sympathy or charity. Nor is justice the sole political value. Whatever justice is, it is not the same as liberty, obligation, or equality, although it may involve them and promote them. There are limits to justice, then, however broad its reach and however frequent its sway.

But precisely what is justice is our central concern and we cannot answer that query simply by pointing out the limits of its reach in morality and in politics. As with all key terms in political morality, the truth is that thoughtful people have now as always contrasting and frequently conflicting definitions of what constitutes justice. Plato was a great theorist of justice in ancient Athens, but so was Aristotle, and they did not agree on what justice was. Both argued that it involved rendering to each person what is their due, but Plato felt that what was due to each of us varied enormously, according to our wisdom and our innate talents, while Aristotle was far more impressed with a concept of justice that involved treating people equally when they were equals and unequally when they were not. Aristotle also thought justice partly involved the operations of law and punishment, while Plato denounced the law and law courts and insisted that law always frustrated justice.

In the nineteenth century as well, many thinkers debated the question of the nature of justice. For example, Jeremy Bentham and Karl Marx both developed intelligent and perceptive theories, but they did not agree. Bentham argued that justice was served when the greatest good for the greatest number was the principle that ruled society, while Marx insisted that to each according to his needs was the essence of justice. Today the arguments go on as they must, since justice is so important a matter. Black militants who demand compensation to blacks for past injustices clash with white "hardhats" who contend that such compensation is unjust for them; welfare mothers assert that justice requires that their support payments increase while hardpressed middle-class taxpayers shout that justice mandates no more taxes; a pacifist says that justice does not allow any more wars, while most international relations professors defend the idea of the just war.

This chapter considers justice in the light of several widely accepted answers to the quandaries of justice. We present these viewpoints on justice, probe their respective strengths and weaknesses, and then we suggest a resolution to the age-old conundrum in political life: "What is justice?" Specifically, we look at four visions of justice. First, we consider definitions that locate justice in natural or divine laws, rather than human ones. These views argue that higher laws are the standard for what is justice and that the just person attempts to adhere to them as perfectly as he or she can. Second, we explore the familiar perspective that justice exists in statute law or in a set of procedures that are intrinsic to law as we know it in the Anglo-American world. According to this idea, the just citizen is one who follows the law and the just law or legal decision is one that accords every person due process of law. Third, we examine concepts of justice that derive from considerations of utility, of what is the greatest good for the greatest number. Bentham was only one of many thinkers who argue that the just society is one that seeks the general public good as its primary goal, while defining the just citizen as one who cares about the greatest good above all else. While some utilitarians virtually equate justice and the greatest happiness (utility) principle, others say that utility is not justice itself but superior to it and a valuable replacement for it. A comparison between J. S. Mill and Bentham, respectively, in this regard is instructive. In this context we also briefly consider the work of the celebrated modern theorist of justice, John Rawls. Finally, we look at what we call the ordinary language definitions of justice, those that see justice as what is rightfully due to people, including such ideas as merit, effort, equality, or need. These four items require considerable discussion because we use some or all of them whenever we speak of justice, and because in a combination of them probably lies the proper standard of justice.

Divine and Natural Justice

Perhaps the oldest view about justice is that justice is found in laws that are natural or divine in origin rather than man made. An ancient example of a divine conception can be found in the Old Testament's Law of Moses, the Ten Commandments. According to the Old Testament, faithful adherence to the Commandments is God's will for mankind and guarantees the just life. A quite different, and more contemporary, example of a divine standard of justice may be found in the speeches and pamphlets of such civil disobedients as Martin Luther King, Jr. and pacifist Quakers. They repeatedly violated the laws of governments in the name of the laws of transcendental justice. Like Moses before them, they have argued that justice is not for man to determine, nor is it the province of human laws unless they accurately reflect divine will. Justice is of God and His ways.[1]

Other thinkers have sometimes stressed a similar criterion of natural justice, that there are natural laws that provide humans with the appropriate norms of justice. For example, Henry David Thoreau approved both nonviolent and violent acts in defiance of government, asserting that the laws of nature were far superior for the soul who sought to live rightly and be just. Many nineteenth-century anarchists such as Peter Kropotkin, the Russian, claimed that governments and their laws always violated the justice that could only be achieved under the guidance of the laws of natural order. Many conservative thinkers such as Russell Kirk call on natural laws in order to argue that one must obey man-made rules, yet even they have clearly placed natural or divine rules above all others. Finally, many of those today who are most concerned about the environment, ecology, and the energy crisis, repeatedly speak in terms that show that they believe we are transgressing implacable natural laws that we ought to follow rather than flaunt.[2]

The enduring emphasis in some areas of Christianity on divine laws, the interest in the environmental movement in natural laws, and the persistence in traditional Africa and modern Islam of divine regulations all remind us today that the appeal to natural or divine standards of justice is by no means a phenomenon of the past. Yet it is also true that most Western philosophers and most Americans do not seem to think or talk in these terms about justice very often any more. This is due partly to a widespread, though hardly unanimous, decline of confidence in this age of skepticism that there is a divine or natural standard of justice. Partly it is also due to the relative remoteness of religious faiths to the politics of even the most ardent believers. The example of King and of thousands of religious conscientious objectors to the Vietnam war teaches us, however, of the other side, of the many for whom justice is not ours to define or determine, since it lies in the provinces of God or nature. There are still many who glance up to Heaven for their guide to justice.

[1]*Old Testament*, "Deuteronomy" and "Leviticus." M. L. King, Jr., *Why We Can't Wait*, (New York: Signet, 1964).

[2]H. D. Thoreau, *Walden and Other Writings*, (New York: Random House, 1950).

P. Kropotkin, *Mutual Aid*, (New York: McClure, 1907).

R. Kirk, *The Conservative Mind*, (Chicago, Henry Regnery, 1953), Chapter One and conclusion.

Both the divine and the natural approaches to justice are necessarily incomplete as a version of justice unless they include a specific discussion of the substance of justice in each case. The stress on divine rules, as in the Ten Commandments, or on natural ways, as in Thoreau's *Walden*, constitute definite statements of justice because they contain not merely a justification, such as God or nature, but because they also contain a set of substantive rules that outline the forms of justice. Mere stress on justifications whether divine or natural does not get us very far, then, without a corresponding consideration of the substantive principles that accompany a justification of justice. These vary widely within natural or divine justifications. For example, at times the Old Testament makes justice a matter of retribution, whereas the New Testament makes the heart of justice forgiveness. Yet both views have a notion of justice grounded in a divine criterion. The situation is no different among natural theories of justice. The nineteenth-century American, W. G. Sumner, argued that natural justice supports a highly competitive capitalist society where merit was the norm of justice. Thoreau on the other hand, thought the message of nature was equality and need. Thoreau and Sumner agreed on the standard of nature, but disagreed on the substance of what nature teaches.[3]

This problem with these traditional approaches to justice does not rule out theories that employ a divine or natural justification. But it gives us reason to observe that simply stating justice is divine or natural in origin tells us little about the content of justice while at the same time ignoring the multitude of conflicting opinion regarding the content of justice whether divine or natural. The case for justice must be demonstrated, not merely asserted. These differing versions suggest to many people that there may not be a true standard of justice present in nature or the heavens, but it is impossible to prove the truth one way or another.

A related question asks exactly how one finds these higher forms of justice. For Thoreau the answer lay in personal intuition. This approach may be satisfactory for some, but it is certainly true that such a subjective process always reveals so many alternate visions of the truth that one can only be somewhat skeptical of each claim. More frequently, those who look to natural or divine justice see reason as the means that leads upward to truth. Proper reason, sometimes termed right reason, can allegedly open the deepest secrets of the universe. Often long and disciplined study is needed before reason can see the higher truths. This was the view of Plato, but other theorists have believed that right reason was easily available to us all. This was the democratic faith of Jefferson and Paine. In any case, right reason creates the same problem for those who earnestly suggest that it leads us to natural or divine justice. Either right reason is fallible or most people who have used it have been mistaken, since so many differing interpretations of

[3]H. D. Thoreau, *op. cit.*
     W. G. Sumner, *Social Darwinism,* (Englewood Cliffs, N.J.: Prentice-Hall, 1963).

justice crowd the stage competing for billing as the truth discovered by right reason. The great medievalist St. Thomas, the remarkable classical thinker Aristotle, and the modern liberal John Locke all believed in right reason, but the content of what justice was to them varied, and sometimes varied *enormously*. Right reason seems to lead in so many directions that skeptics cannot help but be cautious about affirming that justice is unquestionably divine or natural and right reason tells us so.[4]

Another difficulty exists in a key assumption of many who look to God and right reason for their standard of justice, a problem that is the most basic of all. They take it for granted that determining the proper norm and applying it in a contrary world are the greatest roadblocks they face, but in fact they must also justify their belief that God will inform us about justice. In fact, we may easily believe in God without being sure that he provides us with a ready standard of justice. Because God is in His heaven does not at all mean justice is there as well.

Procedural Justice

Americans are familiar with another concept of justice: legalism or proceduralism—the idea that justice involves guaranteeing due process of law or, more broadly, following the law. We say a just court is one that follows the law in conducting a trial; a jury renders a just verdict when it adheres to the appropriate rules for deciding cases; a policeman gets a warrant before searching our home or else he is violating our legal rights to justice under the Constitution; a citizen acts unjustly when he or she breaks the law by cheating on his income tax.

Those who are sympathetic to procedural justice take for granted that justice involves adhering to law because they assume law embodies by its very nature a set of intrinsic principles or procedures that make it the best possible instrument for individual justice. Obedience to the law ensures justice as long as the law contains these attributes that proponents rate as central to its very being. Laws that lack these features are not really legitimate laws. Lon Fuller terms these standards the "inner morality" of the law, an apt characterization of the proceduralist belief that we obtain moral justice only within a procedurally fair legal system.

Proceduralists like Fuller argue that the uniform and equal application of laws to all citizens is the most important procedural norm. To avoid caprice and arbitrariness is the highest objective of a lawmaker. It is no simple matter to

[4]St. Thomas Aquinas, *The Political Ideas of St. Thomas Aquinas*, (New York: Hafner, 1953).
Aristotle, *The Politics*, (NewYork: Oxford University Press, 1962).
John Locke, *Two Treatises of Government*, (New York: Hafner, 1959).
J. Pieper, *Justice*, (New York: Pantheon Books, 1955).

decide when any law is arbitrary or not, but few would disagree, for example, that the law for murder must be the same for blacks and for whites. Similarly, the law must not discriminate between two people in two identical situations in an inexplicable or illogical manner. If drunks who are picked up on day one end up in jail while those picked up on day two are immediately released, the law on punishment of drunkenness allows capricious and, therefore, unjust results. Proceduralists also denounce arbitrary distinctions in the law whenever they appear if they are based on favoritism in the forms of nepotism, friendship, political association or bribery, and financial gain. All violate justice.

Other aspects of the law that proceduralists often cite as vital to justice include some of the most renowned and treasured provisions of the law as we know it. These features include the norm that the law must be publicized, that it must be clear and understandable, that laws passed today cannot refer to the past, that no one may judge themselves under the law, and that disputes must be resolved quickly for justice to be done. Proceduralists insist that it is obviously unjust to hold people to laws they know nothing about, or to laws that they cannot comprehend. These criteria are simply a matter of giving people a decent chance in life. The prohibition of laws that refer to and apply to past actions is similarly justified. After all, how reasonable is it to punish someone for what he did yesterday when it was perfectly legal? Provisions about a speedy trial and impartial rather than self-interested judgment work in the same direction. Both promote provision of a fair chance for everybody. Long-delayed trials deny fairness as witnesses forget or die and money is endlessly spent for lawyers. Dickens, in his novel *Bleak House,* tells us the unforgettable story of the case of Jarndyce and Jarndyce, a case that never ended but ruined all concerned.[5]

The proceduralist ethic is familiar to us, but it is hardly the only way we think of justice. It is a partial version at best. We all sometimes say that laws are unjust or trial verdicts unjust even though they meet every standard for a procedural justice. The error of those who make the inner rules of law the exclusive content of justice involves a failure to include substantive as well as procedural elements in their definition of justice. Many proceduralists do not appreciate that all the "fair" procedures in the world can conceivably mask purposes implicit in laws that offend our common notions of what is just, because the laws may contain values or be designed for substantive objectives which we would consider unjust. No matter how procedurally fair, laws may consistently downgrade merit or equality or need in their effects, or they may work out in a manner that ensures that some people will be consistent winners and others consistent losers in the social, economic, or political system, inevitably provoking the cry that the laws are flagrantly unjust.

[5]L. Fuller, *The Morality of Law* (New Haven: Yale University Press, 1965).
H. Kelsen, *What Is Justice?* (Berkeley: The University of California Press, 1957).

A second problem with exclusively procedural concepts of justice is that they tend to be based on assumptions that are naive and therefore fundamentally flawed. For example, they are naive about society because they often assume that people have equal resources, or chances, within a legal system when, in fact, they definitely do not. Fair procedures work fairly only when people possess or have access to roughly equal skills in the legal process, skills that often require considerable knowledge and money to obtain. People who have enough education to know how to hire a skilled lawyer to help them in the legal system, as well as people who have plenty of money with which to pay their lawyer well, obviously are in a better position to get procedural justice than the old, sick person living on Social Security, the poor migrant worker, or the ignorant, unskilled ghetto resident. Even when procedures appear to promote justice the poor and undereducated are always at a disadvantage. Only in that society where there are no large numbers of such people is genuine procedural justice likely to exist and our society, like others, is scarcely there yet.

Pure proceduralists are also naive in their hope that their justice will never involve taking sides in ongoing political conflicts. The proceduralists' very emphasis on defining justice in terms of law and its inner rules implies and reinforces a strong bias for the existing political and socioeconomic order. Legal norms are not neutral but are, instead, inevitably conservative in their policy impact. At the least, proceduralists wish to impose on all programs the various proceduralist criteria, a doctrine that enthusiasts for change inevitably find conservative in theory and practice.

These difficulties with a proceduralist view, however, should not lead us to disregard it as a legitimate aspect of an adequate definition of justice. Our later argument will be that justice *does* have to do with law and with "the inner morality" of law, but it has to do with other things as well. The ultimate problem with this concept of justice as with others is that it lays exclusive claim to the totality of justice when it properly constitutes only part of that elusive concept.

We agree with Hobbes and others that the general positive conception of justice as the legal fulfillment of contracts and the provision of a pervasive order for all is important. Justice does include room for good rules and the stability that obeying contracts and rules and state support for them can provide. However, as we argue below, exclusive focus on this (or an even narrower focus on procedures) is an insufficient concept of justice because it fails to take other valid aspects into account. Justice is too rich to be neatly summarized in a single area because the valid but disparate insights of many different thinkers detailed within this chapter cannot be ignored.

Utilitarianism

If two frequent images of justice, legal proceduralism and divine justice, are not broad enough to cover all of justice, other theories claim to be. Perhaps the most influential is the utilitarian theory, which holds that justice is the achievement of the greatest good for the greatest number in a given society. The great developers of this view, British theorists in the eighteenth and nineteenth centuries, including Bentham, John Stuart Mill, and Sidgwick, all ably defended variants of the utilitarian perspective, each modifying and developing it to suit their tastes. Bentham is famous in the history of utilitarianism for his detailed and ultimately fruitless discussion of the meaning and typology of pleasure (good) as well as for his unsuccessful efforts to construct a mechanism, a calculus, for measuring relative pleasure. John Stuart Mill's contribution was his attempt to rank some pleasures over other pleasures, an attempt that led to the idea that some people were morally superior to others. Sidgwick contributed what many think is by far the most sophisticated exploration and defense of the utilitarian view. All of these men and others since, however, always return to hold on to the central ideas of the utilitarian theory of justice.[6]

The common utilitarian theory is that each individual experiences pleasure and pain and seeks happiness by maximizing pleasure and limiting pain. The best utilitarian polity ensures happiness as much as possible by undertaking programs designed to encourage pleasure and reduce pain for the largest possible number of citizens. Utilitarian justice reigns when the political order serves this end for most people and certainly a majority. By its very principle, the just utilitarian government acts in terms of the general population and does not concern itself first of all with each and every individual as an individual with natural or legal rights. Utilitarians are conscious of the dangers posed to the general good by individuals who resist this goal. We agree with them whenever we feel it is necessary to restrain one minority or another, the rights of the minority of murderers to kill, Mormons to have several wives, or government officials to steal. But most of us believe some individual rights must always be protected, especially civil liberties and the right of due process of law. In principle (if rarely in practice) utilitarians do not agree. They argue, for example, that if general benefit would result by reducing crime, the sacrifice of some people's due process of law would be valuable. Drastic proposals for summarily imprisoning drug pushers or addicts often reflect this persuasion.

On the other hand, the utilitarian equation of justice with the greatest good for the maximum number strikes a responsive chord in us as we complain about special advantages the wealthy few obtain in America through inequitable tax laws or "wrist-slap" sentences meted out to corrupt public officials as being unjust. We quickly become disgusted at catering to "special interests" and ignorance of the general good.

Yet our point is that the utilitarian conception of justice is not satisfactory just

[6]J. Bentham, *The Principles of Morals and Legislation* (New York, Hafner, 1948).
J. S. Mill, *Utilitarianism* in *Utilitarianism, Liberty and Representative Government,* (New York: E. P. Dutton and Co., 1951).
H. Sidgwick, *The Methods of Ethics* (London: Macmillan, 1893).

because we can also easily imagine situations where what might be useful for the bulk of society would offend our common sense of individual justice. Utilitarianism enshrines the principles of majority rule to the point of opening the door to tyranny of the majority by its concentration less on one or another individual than on the general body politic. Because it might well be just from a utilitarian point of view to close a troublesome newspaper, persecute a rebellious black minority, or imprison selfish millionaires, most of us would argue that utilitarianism hardly guarantees justice. We remember that the Athenians killed Socrates, convinced that he threatened the general interest of classical Athens, but we intuitively know that this was an egregious injustice. The point is that all of us normally (and rightly) think of justice in terms of individual persons, while utility permits a good many individual injustices, so to say, if they promote the general good. While we may want to agree with many utilitarians that their search for the greatest good for the greatest number is important, we should not automatically confuse it with the essence of justice.

There are several other objections to a utilitarian analysis of justice as well. Utilitarians are more concerned with happiness than they are with strictly ethical issues among which we would usually class justice. Nobody denies that happiness is valuable, but there is no particular reason to equate it with the moral concept of justice. A second argument stresses that utilitarianism is not much good as a criterion of justice because it is impractical. Critics ask how we can measure such vague notions as happiness or pleasure and pain. If we cannot measure them effectively, we cannot discover what the greatest good for the greatest number is—we will not be able to locate justice.

The most celebrated essay on justice in our time, John Rawls' *A Theory of Justice*, also attacks the utilitarian position because it seems quite able to sacrifice justice for individuals in its search for the common good or "justice."[8] Rawls charges that utilitarianism, for example, could quite conceivably support a system of slavery even though few, if any, of us would agree that a system of slavery is just. Like those who look to human, natural or divine laws for justice, Rawls insists that justice requires an independent standard of definition, one free from the utilitarians' tendency to subordinate justice to utility. Rawls' solution is his proposal that justice refers to two basic independent norms. First, he contends that it is about equal liberty for all, and, second, he maintains that it is about equal distribution of goods, as long as equal liberty is not sacrificed and any inequalities exist for the purpose of the benefit of all people, especially the poorest.

There is good reason for agreeing with Rawls that the utilitarian outline for justice is inadequate, but there is less basis for believing that Rawls has resolved the problem of justice in politics. He offers in equal freedom a definition that few of us would quickly recognize as reasonably connected with justice. Freedom, equal or not, clearly seems to be about something other than justice. It is used in different linguistic circumstances than justice is—the free man is not necessarily the just man, nor is a free society necessarily a just society—so that the question becomes why Rawls and others who propose to merge freedom and justice do so. Part of the explanation lies in the tendency of numerous thinkers to associate justice with any or all values they especially honor, since justice from Plato's time onward has often been considered the supreme value in politics. Another reason lies in Rawls' qualification that he seeks *equal* freedom. Equality in freedom or anything else *is* commonly associated with justice and, as we will see shortly, it is a serious and defensible view of justice on its own. But it is one thing to suggest that adequate freedom in a society requires that all citizens must have an equal amount of liberty and quite another to assert that equal freedom is justice. (For an extensive analysis of this point, see Chapters 4 and 5: "Liberty and Equality.")

Rawls' second criterion of justice—his principle of distribution—also seems inadequate. It is more familiar to an ordinary understanding of justice insofar as it stresses that goods should be distributed equally, but Rawls' modification of the norm to allow great inequalities in order to benefit the general population is really a covert form of the utilitarian justice he so vigorously attacks, or at least a relatively minor modification of it. Rawls' motivation for permitting massive inequalities is his belief that they may often rebound to the greatest good for each person. This is not vastly different from the principle of the greatest good for the greatest number, although it is more egalitarian. Rawls believes that strict economic equality will prevent capital formation and thus interfere with normal economic development against the wishes and the self-interest of most people in any society. He may be right but this calculation has little to do with justice and a good deal more to do with the supposed practical necessities of economic development. Rawls and the utilitarians would like the comfortable feeling that justice is useful and practical but there is no necessary connection between what is right and what is practical.[7]

Rendering Each His Own

Sometimes we do think about justice in procedural and legal terms and sometimes in utilitarian ones, but ordinarily we conceive of justice in another way that links justice with rendering what is due to us. When we usually say we have gotten just treatment we mean we believe that we have received what is properly ours, while we feel dealt with unjustly when we do not obtain "what is coming to us."

[7] J. Rawls, *A Theory of Justice*, (Cambridge, Mass.: Harvard University Press, 1971); also see B. Barry, *The Liberal Theory of Justice: A Critical Examination of the Principal Doctrines of A Theory of Justice by John Rawls* (Clarendon: Oxford University Press, 1973).

This common idea of justice makes a good deal of sense. It is built on a model of a world in which people are held to have justified claims and in which justice constitutes respect for those claims. The foundation of this belief and, thus, of the sense of justice, is a root conviction that every person deserves to be considered as a special moral being who must be accorded respect and decent treatment. The implicit assumption is that people should be seen as ends in themselves rather than as mere means to be used and abused as others may see fit. All people are due all of the rights and honors of personhood.

This vision of justice may be illustrated by the following example: when a court passes judgment on two equally guilty defendants in a murder case by freeing A while sending B to jail for twenty-five years, we take it for granted that B has a right to claim he has been unjustly sentenced. We do so because we feel B's claim as a person has obviously received less serious consideration than A's has. Legal proceduralists might say we do so because the legal norm of impartiality has been violated, but the norm of impartiality itself derives from the more fundamental value of respect for persons.

Unfortunately, this example is far too simple in its resolution for most disputes about justice even when we apply the idea that justice is a matter of what is rightfully due us. In fact, few—if any—practical quarrels over justice can be resolved by invoking the formal rule that we should treat people with respect for their claims. The reason is that what it actually means to treat people in this manner is not at all clear when we act in the real world composed of many people with conflicting claims, each clamoring for the justice due to them as people. For instance, would giving each his due imply treating everyone equally as the judge does who sentences the two murderers to jail for the same term? Others would say it involves taking into account the fact that one murderer has a family that he must support while the other does not. They might suggest giving the killer with the greater *need*—to support a family—a shorter sentence. Others would argue that the sentence should turn on the *merit* of the two murderers' previous lives: since A led a decent, hardworking life and killed only in a momentary lapse, A should get only a light sentence. Others might insist that distinctions should be made on the basis of the *contribution* each person has made to society before his crime or by the amount of *work* he does in prison life. Or, consider the case where A gets a higher salary than B because A works harder. Is that just? Would it be just if A got a higher salary because he did better work because he was smarter? Would it be just if B had greater need? Would it be fairer if they both got equal salaries regardless of work, merit or need?

Clearly what is owed to us as people is *not* self-evident. We must probe each of the several classic positions that attempt to provide an answer before we can weave a solution that will direct us at last to a satisfactory conception of the elusive concept of justice.

What Is Due To Us Defined By Desert or Merit

A very frequent test for determining justice as what is due to us is merit or desert. The general notion is that we receive justice when we are rewarded in one way or another according to what we are or do in life as opposed to what we need or to simple equality. Surely, this view suggests, the productive worker deserves more salary than his hardworking but incompetent fellow employee. Similarly, it contends that the decent law-abiding citizen deserves more respect than the criminal.

There are actually two forms of this argument, although in practice they are often mixed or confused together. One version contends that merit should depend on one's personal qualities rather than achievements, on one's intelligence or character or moral virtue. It holds that a just society would honor these characteristics—the human being's best features—and thereby demonstrate great respect for humanity. The other version concentrates on what people achieve, believing that contribution or productivity in life is a better basis for justice than any traits or talents one happens to have.

If we were to ask, for instance, what the desert test would define as a just economic distribution, the answer would depend on how we define desert. If we were to apply the productivity criterion, justice would involve rewarding those who were the most successful at their jobs. This is the principle of justice that supposedly operates in capitalist economic systems, except insofar as union seniority rules modify the rule in some cases. It is the usual standard for awarding grades in our universities, in deciding which sports players deserve the greatest respect, and in deciding which politicians deserve reelection. There is no doubt, then, that this criterion of justice is one that is common to our way of thinking and talking about the subject; at least as common, indeed, as any other definition. On the other hand, desert defined by moral virtue or intelligence, which might well lead to a curious outcome in which the most powerful people might be priests or intellectuals, is hardly as popular.

Neither of these two desert formulas is really satisfactory as a *sole* ground for justice in society, no matter how often we may think either is an appropriate standard. What we are or achieve depends to a large extent on chance, heredity, personal background, and general social conditions. This is so pervasive that it is scarcely fair to give people vastly differential rewards exclusively on the basis of "merit." Why should it be just to reward one man with money, status, or power disproportionately to others in similar situations because one is born brighter than another or had access to a better education or because he is more productive at work when he was born more talented or happens to have access to superior training? The same point may be made another way by noting that advocates of the merit principle of justice seem to assume that everyone has an equal opportunity and it is therefore only just that those who succeed should do so. The truth is that powerful hereditary and environmental factors block the possibility of equal chances and call into question the definition of justice as "merit."

How far should we carry this skepticism of the role of our choices in structuring where we end up in life? It suggests a framework of determinism in life and forgets that, after all, people do sometimes "overcome"—as we say—their up-bringing or surmount some amazing hereditary handicaps. It also overlooks the fact that it usually takes a good deal of effort to realize even the most innate abilities. It is fair to conclude that it is not self-evident that all variations in what people accomplish are simply a matter of their environmental and hereditary background for which they deserve no credit. There does often seem to be some "justice" to people's success or failure but the problem is that it is almost impossibly difficult to determine exactly what proportion of anyone's achievement is due to his or her own choices and efforts. Devising a workable standard of measurement for an entire society would be even harder, perhaps impossible.

While it may well be impossible to establish how much of our success we "deserve," it is clear that the idea that human work or enterprise should be so important is actually a third type of the merit theory of justice. Appealing as the idea is to us that we should be rewarded for what efforts we make, this approach does not entirely escape the general problem for all versions of the desert test—the question of the role of heredity and environment. Even if we take a pure form of the criterion and decide that it is just to reward people only on the basis of the work they put in regardless of what is produced in the end, as in the case where the student tells the professor he merits a high grade on a bad term paper because he worked hard on it or in the case where people on welfare are criticized for "getting something for nothing," we are not out of the woods. We still cannot avoid the factor of environment. The efforts we make in our jobs, or whatever we do, are not exclusively our independent doing. Our socialization, our family, our upbringing, and our general social surroundings have a great deal to do with our attitudes toward work and effort in life. Nor can we find a practical means to uncover what in our efforts is due to our choices and what comes from our background.

A second kind of doubt about the desert view directs our attention to its implications when it is carried out to its logical conclusion. A thorough desert model of justice challenges both democratic political equality and equality before the law. Desert invoked in politics might mean that only the best minds or the most productive economic entrepreneurs should rule, whereas traditional democratic theory hold that *regardless* of merit every person should have an equal political voice. Desert might also mean that the "virtuous"—or the most economically valuable citizens—should get favored treatment in the courts, whereas the legalist conception of justice maintains that there ought to be equal protection of the laws for all people, good and bad, productive or unproductive, hardworking or lazy. Advocates of a desert theory of justice, of course, rarely plan to apply the merit position to either the political or legal realms but it is worth noting how elitist the merit theory is, and we cannot avoid wondering why one aspect of life should be governed by desert and another by equality, especially when merit advocates really believe that justice can be found only in the desert test.

We make a third argument about the merit test by observing the curious fact that underneath its praise of talent or accomplishment is an implicit set of standards for what constitutes "good" abilities or "genuine" achievement. Proponents of merit certainly do not think it is just for society to reward either people who have unusual ability at fleecing the unsuspecting poor out of their money or organized crime "hit men" who are skilled at eliminating troublesome competitors. Nor do they have much admiration for those whose achievements depart from the boundaries drawn by the conventional moral pieties of society. In other words, just any talent and just any achievement rarely merits admiration or is called just. Usually an implicit utilitarian or "public good" standard may be found acting to distinguish good and bad talent or accomplishment. Insofar as this is the case, the question becomes whether or not the merit test is a suppressed form of the utilitarian theory of justice and, therefore, vulnerable to all the objections we raised about that view.

Proponents of the merit test insist that critics fail to understand two points, first that judgments based on merit are an inevitable feature of existence because social differentiation will not go away and, second, that society needs to reward people of unusual capacities and productiveness, because if it does not, then rapid decline will occur. These empirical contentions may or may not be sound, but they do not establish a case for a desert theory of justice. After all, justice is a moral concept. It is about what ought to be and the fact that it may run head on into empirical or pragmatic realities does not necessitate a definition of justice that will perfectly accommodate them. What ought to be and what is or what is pragmatic are often in tension and there is no particular harm to that. One may choose to have economic inequality for the practical reason that it may provide incentives for greater production of goods but this choice does not require us to agree that justice is based on desert as much as it reminds us of the significant truth that justice is one value among many and not necessarily the value a society will, or should, rank highest.

In the end, the greatest puzzle about a desert conception of justice does not derive from all the arguments and counterarguments we have examined so far. It lies in the question of whether or not there is an appropriate distinction between what a person is or does as an individual—and therefore merits—and the person as a member of the human race. Is the idea of justice, which is about what is owed to a person, to be grounded in the person as person, regardless of all else, or is it to be based in what the person as an individual has achieved by one measure or another as compared with other individual people? This is the great issue between the desert theory of justice and its classic opponent, the equalitarian position, which we examine next.

We should note before hand, however, that many desert theories of justice are careful to construct a quite sophisticated system where they insist on merit qualifications for justice in some cases and equalitarian qualifications for others. Following Aristotle's classical argument, they devise a formal standard, which states that equals should be treated equally and unequals unequally. This means that where people are fundamentally the same, as for example as citizens, they receive justice only when they get equal consideration. For example, they all deserve "equal protections of the laws" and all should have an equal right to vote and to participate politically. Yet where people are unequal, as in their economic productive capacity or in their basketball talent, justice requires they be dealt with on their merits. This modified form of the desert test meets our earlier point, which suggested that a pure merit test is enormously vulnerable to accepting drastic political and legal inequalities—injustices, we might say. It also meets criticism that the desert theory never demonstrates sufficient respect for what is due to people as people, regardless of what they do, regardless of their acquired characteristics, and natural strengths.

This mixed view suffers from a serious internal flaw, however, because it depends on a confidence that we can say when people are equal and when they are unequal even though this assumption is highly doubtful. It may seem to be a matter of fact that people are equal (or should be) in their role as citizens or before the law. But this is no more than a statement of faith or value, from which many thinkers from Plato to Nietzsche have vigorously dissented. Beyond this problem, however, we observe that as long as this understanding of justice is largely a desert theory, it still must confront all the serious reservations that can be expressed about any merit approach. It goes part of the way toward a more adequate view, but only part of the way.[8]

What is Due to Us Defined as Equality

The egalitarian position holds that justice demands that each of us be treated equally above all else because we are all equal members of the human race. Two senses of equality are usually meant: equality of consideration and equality of treatment. What is not ordinarily implied, however, is the idea that we should be always treated *identically,* for most egalitarians realize that treating people equally need not mean ignoring inevitable human variations. For instance, if one man is a robber, to treat him as a robber does not mean all people should be punished, just that as a person a robber deserves treatment that is

---

[8]S. I. Benn and R. S. Peters, *The Principles of Political Thought,* (New York: The Free Press, 1959).
C. Perelman, *Justice* (New York: Random House, 1967).
C. J. Friedrich and J. Chapman, Editors, *Justice* (New York: Atherton, 1963).

similar to other robbers and yet does not deny his humanity. Yet the thrust of the equalitarian notion *is* toward a vast expansion of the situations in which we would accord people *identical* treatment, especially in the area of incomes, status, and social conditions. . . . "social justice." Supporters of the equality test claim that only this direction adheres to the ideal of rendering respect for individual persons regardless of their multiple talents and backgrounds. They contend that if we genuinely respect people we must respect them regardless of everything else except their very personhood. They argue that the humblest worker and the greatest captain of industry, the most ruthless academic entrepreneur and the most devoted college teacher are the same in what should count in life—their common humanity—and therefore each should get the same honor and income, as well as their present supposedly equal vote and equal courtroom justice.

In our time and place this egalitarian perspective on justice inevitably seems radical. And it is. It has long been the doctrine of many political and economic revolutionaries whose cry for "social justice" has rung loudly in almost all recent revolutions from the Bolshevik revolution in 1917 to the Cuban revolution of the 1960s. But it has also been the doctrine of many thinkers and activists who are hardly violent revolutionaries, men in America like Michael Harrington whose "discovery" of poverty in the United States in the 1960s has much to do with the late War on Poverty and men in Europe like Albert Camus who saw the dangers of revolutionaries and the impossibility of full equality, but who urged his age toward a more egalitarian world.

The egalitarian theory seems radical because it clashes so sharply with the merit test of justice that we apply in art, sports, income, and much else in our society. But we should remember that it is hardly entirely foreign to us since it underlies our understanding of what is just in political life, where we believe each should count as one and only one. Even outside of the strictly political relationships, egalitarian justice may appeal to us whenever we begin to wonder about the great inequalities around us and ask if their existence is just.

At the least everyone must contemplate the gap between the two offspring of our formal principle of justice—equality and desert—and wonder which is right. We certainly cannot forget that desert has substantial weaknesses, as egalitarians are quick to point out, especially its tendency to call social and economic relationships that may have more to do with differences in natural gifts or family environment than anything else.

However, the drawbacks to a concept of justice defined in an egalitarian framework are weighty in their own right. Egalitarians tend to assume that things can be divided up into fair shares in this world. Some, like income, undoubtedly can be, but all jobs are not going to be equally good, all farmland equally rich, all schools equally effective. Some worry that egalitarians do not understand the costs that would be involved in the massive income redistribution that would be required in the United States or Western Europe to begin to approach their goal. Would the typical, relatively peaceful political system survive such a dramatic experiment? A third pragmatic doubt derives from the ancient dilemma between an equally divided but fixed pie versus an unequally divided but steadily increasing pie with greater slices for all or almost all. Critics of egalitarian justice fear that as an economic policy it will eliminate economic incentives and thus actually deny increased life chances for most people that could be insured if there were income differentials to spur the most creative and productive forward. What is the advantage for all people if we are equal in poverty?

These pragmatic criticisms of the egalitarian approach to social justice are common, but egalitarians insist that they are not fatal to their position. They deny the pessimistic prognosis that their opponents often foresee for radical changes, and they never fail to remind their critics of what they consider to be the enormous human costs of the present inegalitarian social and economic arrangements. They also deny that problems of dividing goods as well as finding non-monetary incentives in a more egalitarian society are insoluble. They tend to be optimistic about what humans can do. They also point out that pragmatic objections to their ideal theory of justice are not the same thing as objections that vitiate their theory of justice in principle. If pragmatic points prove to have weight, then their principle may not be fully realized in any society; yet its moral validity and its guiding influence would remain unaffected.

There are more theoretical worries about the egalitarian standard. For example, there is the matter of how far even the most devoted defender of the equality theory of justice would take the ideal. Would anyone seriously propose that justice exists where we all were equally tortured, including the torturers? Would we claim it was just if we all were robbed as long as we all lost an equal amount? Would it be a just polity if we all surrendered our polictical rights to the same (complete) extent? Justice surely does not mean equality in things that somehow violate the formal standard of due respect to all, as torture, robbery, and the absence of political rights would.

On the other hand, a poor objection, if one that some egalitarians open themselves to, is the objection that doubts if egalitarians really mean to give everyone equal salaries, regardless of their varying numbers of children, their medical expenses, or other needs. This skepticism is natural in many cases because too many egalitarians talk of equality as if they meant that everyone should receive the identical income, for example. This tone partly derives from the egalitarian attacks on the enormous inequalities to be found everywhere in modern societies, a tone that may seem to suggest that their solution is always strict formal equality. There is, certainly, no doubt of the egalitarians' belief in equality, but when one examines their argument closely, one finds that rarely do they favor a rigid, formal equality apart from needs. Instead, most egalitarians define equality as a supple and individualized ideal that seeks to make each of us equal in the fundamental aspects of life by distributing income, health care, and the like according to our needs, so that we have substantive, real-life equality rather than a formal equality which is often inequality in practice. This means that we must now look at another but obviously closely related theory of justice: the need theory.[9]

What Is Due To Us Defined as Recognition of Need

The French socialist, Louis Blanc, first advanced need as a type of egalitarian justice in the nineteenth century. Karl Marx was its most famous exponent; his vision of the just social order in the *The Gotha Program* provided for distribution to "each according to his needs."[10]

The need approach is a form of the egalitarian position because needs are ordinarily understood as universal to all people and those whose needs are not being fulfilled therefore lack the equal respect due to all people. This notion of justice today is applied in many places where Karl Marx has never been heard of and in ways and manners that have nothing to do with what he would like or appreciate. This view lies behind such laws as the minimum wage or the provision of welfare payments to the poor in a host of regimes, capitalist or socialist. Proponents of both policies believe that poorly paid workers, or the poor in general, do not receive just treatment if their level of existence falls short of our notions of what is fitting for all human beings. This constitutes an application of a need criterion of justice.

Proponents of the need criterion believe that what counts in determining justice is not formal equality, although they resist any large inequalities, but instead, equality of positive fulfillment of needs. For them equality means equal fulfillment of needs that necessarily are unequal among different people in different times. The needs of a bachelor and the head of a household of five are obviously not the same, and genuine equality will require quite different incomes in the two cases. Similarly, the educational needs of two children who are equally bright but differ tremendously in self-confidence, will vary greatly. The student without self-confidence will require far more attention in order to obtain an equal education.

Certainly need must be taken seriously as a view of justice, for it is more effective than formal equality in accomplishing their joint goal—substantive equality. It is also convincing in its belief that if justice concerns rendering what is due to people, we must measure those claims in terms of actual human needs. Yet there are, as with all theories of justice, noteworthy problems. For one thing,

---

[9]H. Bedau, Editor, *Justice and Equality*, (Englewood Cliffs, N.J.: Prentice-Hall, 1971).
  F. Olafsen, Editor, *Justice and Social Policy*, (Englewood Cliffs, N.J.: Prentice-Hall, 1961).
  R. Brandt, Editor, *Social Justice*, (Englewood Cliffs, N.J.: Prentice-Hall, 1962).
[10]K. Marx, *The Marx-Engels Reader* (New York: W. W. Norton, 1973).

many needs may be hard to satisfy. This is especially true with such psychic needs as love or belonging. But even economic needs cannot be swiftly fulfilled except in societies with considerable abundance, for where needs exceed what is available to distribute, need will be of little use as a mechanism to determine justice. Second, there is the genuine possibility that in rich nations a need standard may encourage all sorts of socially disadvantageous phenomena, particularly if the material aspects of need are given prominence, such as large families, hypochondriacs, and obese people, all able to indulge their "need."

The great problem raised here is the definition of an authentic need. Should need be defined in terms of personal desire, or should society set up so-called objective rules for what constitutes legitimate needs? Clearly need is a vague and elastic concept, for there is no self-evident definition of what need means for people in common or individual terms. Nor does it appear possible to arrive at some magical solution by uncovering a scientific definition of human needs, for what people need is a normative question that depends on what goals people seek. Even elementary needs like food or shelter depend on the acceptance of the normative goal of life, something many thousands of suicides reject each year.

One way to come to terms with what need should be is to distinguish so-called basic needs from the rest of human needs. While basic needs are not intuitively obvious either, if we adopt the objective of the maintenance of a functioning life as our basic value, we can select those needs whose absence would manifestly cause unmistakable harm to people. These would include adequate food, shelter, clothes, and medical care. Agreement that everyone ought to have these things is widespread throughout the world today and its acceptance illustrates the vitality of the need conception of justice at this time. Thoroughgoing enthusiasts for the need test, however, want to go far beyond a minimum needs theory of justice and seek to apply it to all aspects of society's decisions. Hope for any agreement on criteria fades before varying individual preferences. Nor can we blink at the possibility that varying needs may bring social and interpersonal conflicts. I may "need" peace and quiet and you may "need" to practice your electric guitar and it will not always be possible to reconcile our differences. The fact remains, also, that even in rich nations many noneconomic needs simply cannot be satisfied.

Critics of a need theory of justice also worry about two other problems. As with a formal egalitarian concept of justice, they fear that the need test may fail to provide incentives in order to encourage people to continue working, a social need without which no society can long endure and few personal needs be met. If society is founded on the ideal that it exists to meet our needs, who will bother to work if they can get their needs fulfilled without working? This objection does not last into the long run, for if people stop working there will be no means to fulfill their needs. The possible short-run danger exists, but advocates of the need approach hope that people will go on working, or can be convinced to go on working, for community goals or for personal satisfaction. Second, critics challenge us to ponder how far we really believe in the idea that it is just that needs be fulfilled. They suggest that we can all think of needs that people may have to which we do not wish to respond, much less encourage. Do we really want to assist the burglar or the rapist to answer the demands of their powerful yet socially dangerous needs? We will have to agree on a common definition of needs. Certainly this could be done, especially if it was the basic goal of the maintenance of life itself. It we did, then there would be no problem denying the "needs" of the criminal and the burglar and the rapist.[11]

TOWARD RESOLUTION

Each of the theories of justice we have examined has its merits and each vision has considerable plausibility. Few do not have a place when we envision justice in one situation or another. All of them are fallible, however, and none seems to us able to stand alone as a complete theory of justice. This truth provides us with the clue toward a resolution of a satisfactory definition of justice. It tells us that perhaps some combination of definitions of justice promises to bring us closer to our goal of a strong and defensible idea of justice. We want to argue, specifically, that need, utility, equality and merit all have valid associations with the norms and contexts of justice. Though we believe need is its most important single principle, even it cannot stand alone much more effectively than the others. Yet need, much more than a strict and formalistic equality, comes closest to justice understood as rendering what is due to us as human persons, since only need allows for the fact that to achieve substantive equality among human beings and thus equal respect, we will have to afford different services and different degrees of service to individuals. Hopefully this policy will assist people by granting them greater opportunities to develop themselves, authentically pursuing individual talents and interests.

Yet need must be modified as a norm of justice by three other principles. It should be watched over by social utility that we may elect to consider a standard of justice. A conception of the general public good, such as the value of life, will be necessary to select among competing needs, to deny the "needs" of people in clearly antisocial cases, such as the "needs" of pathological murderers and to guard against the abuse of legitimate needs such as is perpetrated by hypochondriacs.

The standard of strict equality must also modify need in the case of political

[11]See footnotes 9 and 10 above.

influence. Equal political opportunity may be hard to achieve, but it should be defended as a goal insofar as politics should serve people and not the reverse. Equality should also be maintained in the application of laws in and out of the courtroom, since this, too, is at the very heart of the democratic faith that celebrates each man and woman as members of the human race. Many argue that the same goal should be pursued in regard to incomes also, either as a matter of justice or as a measure designed to promote genuine political equality, but we contend that incomes should be viewed in a needs framework, because only need can guarantee the substantive equality that is so much of what justice is about.

Finally, there is little doubt that despite its flaws merit plays a large part in our normal, linguistic perceptions of justice. There is no reason why it should not continue to be our operational standard of justice in numerous private areas of life from baseball rules to artistic recognition. Yet when it comes to politics or social and economic policy we doubt that it can legitimately serve as a substitute for egalitarian or needs standards without vitiating our argument that justice must, above all, involve respect for each of us as human beings, regardless of our accidental talents or backgrounds.

Our conclusion, then, is that no single formula explains justice properly. Justice has several sides and several different visions of justice must be included in an adequate understanding of the word. Nor do we claim that we have solved all the ancient riddles that surround the nature of justice. Our point has been to illustrate the many common images of justice that we employ, to explain the meaning, implications, strengths, and weaknesses of each view and to stimulate thought about the concept that we use so often. There is no doubt that wrestling with justice is like trying to climb a greased pole. Yet politics is too often concerned with the rhetoric and reality of justice for any of us to seek to escape this greasy pole.

SUGGESTIONS FOR SUPPLEMENTARY READING

General

Brandt, R., Editor, *Social Justice*, (Englewood Cliffs, N.J.: Prentice-Hall, 1962).
Friedrich, C. J. and J. Chapman, Editors, *Justice*, (New York: Atherton, 1963).
Olafsen, F., Editor, *Justice and Social Policy*, (Englewood Cliffs, N.J.: Prentice-Hall, 1961).
Perelman, C., *Justice*, (New York: Random House, 1967).

Divine and Natural Justice

Pieper, J., *Justice,* (New York: Pantheon Books, 1955).
Aristotle, *The Politics,* many publications.
Plato, *The Republic,* many publications.

Procedural and Legalistic Justice

Fuller, L., *The Morality of Law,* (New Haven: Yale University Press, 1965.)
Kelsen, Hans, *What Is Justice?* (Berkeley: The University of California Press, 1957).

Utilitarianism

Bentham, Jeremy, *The Principles of Morals and Legislation,* many publications.
Mill, John Stuart, *Utilitarianism* (New York: E. P. Dutton and Company, 1951).

Rawls

Rawls, John, *A Theory of Justice,* (Cambridge, Mass.: Harvard University Press, 1971).
Barry, B., *The Liberal Theory of Justice: A Critical Examination of the Principal Doctrines of A Theory of Justice by John Rawls,* (Clarendon: Oxford University Press, 1973).

Merit, Equality, Need

Bedau, Hugo, Editor, *Justice and Equality,* (Englewood Cliffs, N.J.: Prentice-Hall, 1971).
Benn and Peters, *The Principles of Political Thought,* (New York: The Free Press, 1959).
Cahn, E., *The Sense of Injustice,* (New York: New York University Press, 1949).
Ginsberg, M., *On Justice in Society,* (Baltimore: Penguin Books, 1965).
Marx, Karl, *Critique of the Gotha Program,* many publications.

Political
Obligation

Political obligation concerns what duties the citizen owes to the political system in which he lives and what duties it owes to him. It includes the issue of when obedience or disobedience to a political community is morally appropriate. Whenever we ask "Should I obey this law?" or "Do I have a right to disobey my government?" or "When am I obligated to the political community in which I live?" we have begun to be theorists of political obligation and our individual answers to these important and disturbing questions constitute our own theory of political obligation. Our own answers, no matter how simple or complicated, are part of a tradition of concern about political obligation that began with Socrates facing death in the Athens of early fourth century, B.C., and that continues to motivate and puzzle thoughtful people today.

We have every reason to believe that there will be no diminution in the future of the occasions in which people have found themselves confronted with agonizing decisions regarding their political obligations. Certainly recent years have seen many examples of difficult challenges posed to ethical people concerned about the proper ground for obedience or disobedience to the state. For example, many draft-aged men in the years 1967–1971 self-consciously faced excruciating moral problems of political obligation over whether or not they

should answer the U.S. government's draft notices to fight in the Vietnam war. The several thousands of young men who fled to Canada or who went to jail rather than serve in Vietnam, plus many more who elected to serve in the Army, were usually young men who experienced the enduring question of the legitimate basis for political obligation in as acute a form as is imaginable. Many of them did the best they could to work out a personal answer and, while their conclusions differed, anyone in American colleges in those years remembers the endless, intense discussions over political obligation and the Vietnam war, discussions whose consequences are now a permanent part of American history.

This recent experience in our own history suggests that perhaps it will always be true that war is especially likely to test political loyalties and to stimulate profound thought on the subject of political obligation. Loyalty and obligation in wartime affect people so directly, sometimes demanding their lives, and it is hardly surprising that the possibility of losing or giving one's life has a certain tendency to stimulate philosophical reflection! Certainly in the past, war has often been the setting for statements of political obligation. The English civil war of the seventeenth century was the vital context for Thomas Hobbes' classic defense of political obedience, while Edmund Burke's great conservative theory of obligation was written in an England that he believed to be endangered by a France in the throes of revolution and war in the late eighteenth century. But war does not only bring forth the most energetic *affirmations* of political obligation, as we remember when we think of Thoreau in jail for refusing to acknowledge any obligation to support our government in the Mexican-American War (which he contended was fought to promote the evils of slavery) or of the multitude of pacifists in human history who chose to disobey their governments rather than kill men. War is both the pacifist's and the patriot's hour.

In or out of wars, it has also been true that groups as well as individuals have faced crises that raise complex issues of political obligation. From the problems the first Christians faced with imperial Rome until now, an obvious case in point has been the clash between religious movements or churches and their respective political communities. In the United States there has been a continuing conflict between the Amish who have wished to educate their own children and states that denied them this "right," there has been the ongoing, protest of pacifist Quakers who resist the draft and warmaking national governments and there was the great struggle in the late nineteenth century between the polygamist Mormons and a monogamist state and society. All of these conflicts have produced disobedience and all have challenged operative conceptions of political obligation. They also demonstrate lucidly that moral perplexities over adherence to laws or governments often occur in situations in which there are multiple obligations. Moral life in the state as well as elsewhere can be complex, one may be pulled in many directions by felt or real commitments to one's religion, family, friends, principles, or state. When these multiple commitments do not join to reinforce the demands of a political order, then the strength or, ultimately, the validity of one's customary sense of political obligation may be undermined and then *tested*. So it has been sometimes with Amish, Quakers, and Mormons.

Political obligation also inevitably looms up when groups seek to be *included* in a political order, rather than to have a state respect another obligation they may have. Much of the black civil rights movement has illustrated the fact that repeated denials of political obligation, considerable civil disobedience and general assaults on the traditional political order can derive from a desire to have equal rights in a political system. Martin Luther King, Jr. was a recent example of a black thinker and activist who repeatedly talked in terms of the appropriate conditions of political obedience and disobedience as he sought to press the case for blacks in American life. From one angle too, the American Civil War may be seen as a battle over political obligation, over whether slaves should be citizens, with political rights and obligations, as well as over the secessionists' belief that they owed no obligation to the central government of the United States.

Another pointed form of obligation dilemma rooted in a group framework is sometimes posed by the experiences of prisoners of war. While in Vietnam, American prisoners of war generally seem to have remained committed to their political obligation to the United States while not jeopardizing obligations they had to their fellow prisoners or their families at home, this was often not possible for American POW's in the Korean war. The severe conditions of imprisonment in the Korean war and an uneasy combination of selfish expediency, desire to be loyal to collaborating fellow prisoners and a sense of higher loyalty to their own families, explained the extensive collaboration that took place there. This experience indicated once again that multiple obligations may lead to a crisis in political obligation, since some of the Korean collaboration was done in return for messages being sent to prisoners' families, or simply to get home alive to those waiting families.

Today the frequency of conflict and tension over political obligation also arises in situations involving entire peoples rather than specific individuals or selected groups, especially in the cases of colonial or conquered peoples. An examination of the colonial literature before the American Revolution affords a fascinating example of the process by which one people reluctantly challenged their relationship with their founding nation. From 1765 to 1766 colonial pamphleteers moved from the status of increasingly discontented but still loyal citizens to a stance that denied any political obligation to Britain—a dramatic and drastic alteration of their views. This process has been simpler, but no less dramatic for peoples seeking self-determination more recently, such as the host of former British, French, or Belgian colonies in Africa. With some exceptions, Third World theorists had never acknowledged any political obligation to their imperial rulers, and consequently they had a shorter intellectual road to travel to rebellion. But, in the end, many Third World arguments were quite similar to those of the American revolutionary thinkers to the considerable degree that they stressed that colonial people should be free of rulers to whom they owed no moral allegiance or political obligation.

Citizens of nations that have a more immediate experience of political independence, yet fall to conquering armies, such as happened in Western Europe during World War II, must also confront the painful quandry of political obligation. Each citizen, but also the whole nation, must decide at heart to whom they are loyal. The famous French resistence in World War II like the inglorious Vichy collaboration were both statements about political obligation.

In short, from the day Socrates had to decide whether he was obligated enough to the Athenian state in 399 B.C. to give up his life at its command until our own turbulent age, the issue of political obligation has intruded on individuals, groups, and whole nations.

I

GENERAL CHARACTERISTICS OF POLITICAL OBLIGATION

Like any truly serious matter, political obligation is not a simple matter nor is it one that everyone has interpreted in the same way. While there are different conceptions about when people owe or do not owe political obedience to a political order, most discussions start, as ours must, with four general defining points. First, we must be clear that political obligation has to do with ethics, with what is morally right to do. Whether political obligation is practical or impractical, convenient or inconvenient, is secondary to the standard of right that underlies a given theory of political obligation. Some views link political obligation to human desires, others to natural laws, still others to contracts made, but all agree that the matter is ethical.

Second, most contemporary thinkers contend that political obligation must be rooted in human choices. They suggest that people may be obligated or not obligated politically only when they have chosen their obligation commitments. Most theorists of political obligation insist that political obligation like all ethical concepts obtains meaning only in a context in which human choice and personal morality are indissolubly linked, because only when morality is chosen, can people be held responsible for what they do and therefore be treated as dignified individuals. This idea of a responsible, choosing individual is the classic ideal of Western morality, and it has been so at least since the beginning of the Judeo-Christian tradition. This is a proposition basic to both consent and utilitarian approaches, but it is true that not all theories of political obligation are built on choice. We will see that a different tradition insists that the crucial question is not choice, but the commands of natural law.

Most modern thinkers in the present day, however, are likely to try and answer the traditional perplexities surrounding the question of whether a citizen should obey, or is obligated, by asking whether a person has chosen his political order—we use the phrase "consent of the governed" in the United States. The degree of choice may be affected by many things, including the range of options, the mix of external restraints on choices or the balance of negatives consequences on several alternatives. The smaller the range of choice, the weightier the restraints and the heavier the negative costs, the weaker the real choice in a situation—and, consequently, the weaker the political obligation. To mention some of the easier cases, it follows that a rich man has more choices than a poor one, a healthy man more than a sick person, an adult more than a child. A final characteristic of an actual choice is its degree of self-consciousness. People who stumble into loyalties, or inherit them, or even never think about them, have scarcely made as willful or potent a choice as someone who knowingly and reflectively acts.

A third dimension of political obligation is that it occurs only in situations of mutuality, when there are people with whom one may conceivably be in moral contact. Obviously Robinson Crusoe, when he was apparently alone on his desert isle, had no political duties. More important, mutuality means that there can be no condition of political owing where there is no political community, however defined, or when members of a state refuse to agree that they might be connected with each other in a manner that would *mandate* obedience under some conditions or other. This spirit of mutuality at some level is basic for the existence of political obligation, because without at least some sense of national, racial, ethnic, or ethical respect among people, genuine moral relations including political obligation make little sense. Nations are like organizations, they die when people in them no longer care for them and their members, or they eke out a morally empty existence under the reign of the sword or spy.

Finally, many conceptions of obligation suggest that not only is genuine political obligation founded in real choice complemented by an attitude of mutuality, but also that it must be a reciprocal, even egalitarian relationship. While this was not always true, for example in feudal society, today obligation is not generally viewed as limited to one group in society, nor as having different ethical weights among otherwise equal citizens, but instead, as a duty that we owe to each other as equal citizens. U. S. citizens, for example, do not normally have differing political duties as citizens nor, in theory, do the nationals of most other countries who share the modern belief that citizenship implies a fundamental equality in rights and duties. One of the most common complaints of men who received their draft notices in the Vietnam years, that young men were being asked to fight a war made by old men, reflected well the characteristic assumption about the equality of political duties sanctioned by many theories of political obligation, and consequently it was a serious objection to that draft, and any draft.

II

THEORIES OF POLITICAL OBLIGATION

When we speak of political obligation, then, we are talking about the relationship between a citizen and his political order, an ethical relationship whose conditions must be in some sense chosen in an atmosphere of mutuality and equality. Yet to understand these points only brings us to the threshold of the actual importance—and excitement—of the topic of political obligation. Generally comprehending what is implied by the term political obligation is by no means the same thing as knowing which specific form of political obligation is the best. It is this second topic that is the heart of the matter for us, because it must be answered to make headway in our search for a moral basis for a reply to the ongoing human query: "When should I obey, when should I disobey?"

Since the subject of political obligation is so important and challenging and has inevitably attracted many able thinkers over the centuries, it is not surprising that there have been many responses to the quest for the ideal understanding of political obligation, its demands, and its limits. Five candidates stand out as the theories that have been the most popular and that illuminate most clearly the serious issues at stake. Some of these five, such as consent and benefit theory are familiar to some extent to many Americans, but we must not ignore others, natural law, tradition and group conceptions of political obligation lest we fail to observe the full range of alternatives debated in the history of political obligation.

Natural Law

Natural law thinkers argue that in order to decide when one should obey, each of us must look to the truths of the broader moral universe in which we dwell. They provide boundaries for political obligation derived from a standard far higher than any which may be developed by individual consent, the wishes of a political majority, personal benefit, or even tradition. Their higher standard is usually divine law, though sometimes it refers to nature apart from any God. In either case, the assumption is that these higher laws set the terms for human ethical relationships, including political obligation.

According to different thinkers, the exact *content* of these binding natural laws as they apply to political obedience or disobedience has often varied, but throughout most of the history of the Western world, the common view was that natural and divine law counseled *obedience* by the citizen to the political order. This was what the divine laws taught Socrates in ancient Athens, this was the central message of traditional Christianity in the hands of St. Paul or St. Augustine and it was the view of the leading American Tory theorist at the time of our revolution, Jonathon Boucher. All agreed that God, or the gods, commanded the duty of loyalty to the state. While there might be some limits, the main *political* injunction was "render unto Caesar." This was a profoundly conservative theory of political obligation.[1]

Yet other versions of divinely-grounded natural laws have led in other directions. Martin Luther King, Jr. believed that Christian natural law prohibited obedience to any state that failed to treat all persons equally, a position that many abolitionists, including Thoreau, Garrison, and John Brown argued a century earlier in the debate over slavery. The implication of their understanding of divine law was hardly conservative. The same is true of the view of Quakers who deny a duty to serve in the military because their notion of divine law rejects killing. Oftentimes, in fact, natural law has been the basis for political revolution, for the idea that there is a higher moral duty to overthrow a given political regime. This is the doctrine of our own Declaration of Independence, which proclaims that the Creator has ordained the natural right to "life, liberty, and the pursuit of happiness" and a regime that denies these rights must be replaced.[2]

The frequent recourse to natural (or divine) standards to define political obligation is not so self-evident an approach, however, that it is not vulnerable to criticism. One objection follows from the multitude of contending versions of the *content* of a higher truth that is supposedly absolute and without question. It asks whether the existence of all these competing perspectives helps anybody in resolving dilemmas of political obligation even as it surely reveals a miasma of confusion both about the nature of the laws of God and what their implications

---

[1]Socrates, *Apology* and *Crito* in *Plato: The Collected Dialogues,* E. Hamilton and H. Cairns, Editors (Princeton, N.J.: Princeton University Press, 1961).

J. Boucher, *A View of the Causes and Consequences of The American Revolution in Thirteen Discourses* (London: G.C. and J. Robinson, 1797).

St. Paul, *Epistle to the Romans,* Chapter 13.

For St. Augustine, see H. Deane, *The Political and Social Ideas of St. Augustine* (New York: Columbia University Press, 1963).

[2]M.L. King, Jr., *Why We Can't Wait,* (New York; Signet Books, 1964).

H.D. Thoreau, *Walden and Other Essays,* (New York; Random House, 1950).

Declaration of Independence.

might be for political duty. The moral cacophony of competing truths we meet in human experience only seems to promote the idea that there is no single answer, only the pluralism of standards, which will not help us much to decide when to obey or to disobey. The gods of St. Augustine of King or Jefferson appear different, and certainly issue differing commands about political obligation, leading the cynic to suggest that transcendant claims are merely rationalizations of selfish whims. Even those with a distaste for the self-indulgence of cynicism are left confused.

Another problem with this perspective is that its assumption of a certain moral standard increasingly washes up against the massive shoals of contemporary skepticism. In our time, the confidence in absolute answers to our questions, the confidence in God or in his unquestioned norms as the scaffolding for human life, seems weaker than ever—for more and more people they have become a standard to which the modern world does not permit them to repair. It takes its toll, although it is true that a theory may be valid even if no one thinks so.

In any case, there always was a peculiar overconfidence among proponents of natural law that, even if there were standards on which everyone could agree, this fact would help us in concrete moral and political decisions. Broad principles, no matter how "natural" or "divine," are not easily translated into specifics. For example, Christians have never been able to agree as to the concrete meaning of the Old Testament injunction "Thou Shalt Not Kill." Did this commandment forbid wars? Leading Catholic thinkers like St. Augustine and St. Thomas repeatedly denied this interpretation, while Quakers and Mennonites defend it. Did this rule forbid capital punishment? Most Christian thinkers, before and after the Inquisition have not thought so, yet others have eloquently disagreed, especially in our age.

Despite these substantial problems, however, today there remain vibrant traditions in political theory and action that continue to insist that religious-based natural law must be the ultimate recourse in questions of political duty, because some people still do believe in the existence and/or the value of ultimate definitions in political and ethical discourse. It may be a matter of faith, but the faith is still alive for some followers of Martin Luther King, Jr., for William F. Buckley, Jr., and for other American conservatives and for radicals like the Berrigan brothers in the Catholic Left. It remains a living option that some thinkers, and activists, still choose and its ultimate validity is not really disprovable, while its consolation of certainty in a complex moral world is substantial.

History and Tradition   A second answer to the puzzles over obedience or disobedience in a political community focuses on the moral weight of historical traditions. Its proponents claim that what is customary or traditional in a society should determine for us the boundaries of political obligations. They argue that human experience, which the past represents, is a sounder guide to the correct path when any great moral decision must be faced than temporary majority sentiment or an individual's opinion could ever be. No greater exponent of this viewpoint ever existed than Edmund Burke, the eighteenth-century British conservative. To him society was a contract between the past, the present and the future, in which all of us were bound together in human custom and experience. To ignore these ties of social history, to ignore our commitments to the past, would be immoral.

Burke's argument appeared as an attack on the French Revolution, which explicitly rejected a Burkean notion of traditional definitions of political obligation, but it continues to be employed today by many American conservatives, such as Buckley or Russell Kirk, in an obviously different environment, often in conjunction with a religious natural law stance. But, more broadly, it is the characteristic of the ardent patriot in every land, who is proud of his country, its accomplishments and its past.[3]

In many other instances the master premise of the traditionalist has less to do with patriotism than with pragmatism. Some theorists like Britain's Michael Oakeshott insist that the past is a better guide for our moral choices in the present and the future than any choices individuals or majorities may make at any given moment because the past reflects a long record of choices and their consequences. This analysis consciously avoids any high-flown moral language, but the concrete significance of their stance is an ethical theory that tradition ought to be followed.[4]

In political terms, most thinkers who employ a traditionalist argument usually conclude that the parameters of political obligation are broad and the bounds of morally permissible disobedience narrow. History, it would seem, usually teaches obedience, although, in fact, what the past of a nation may be said to teach, in anything, is questionable. History, of course, can provide a basis for political *disobligation*, as the Huguenots of France, the American colonists of England or the Leninist sufferers under the Czars perceived their own histories. Our point is that history is a record of many things, and the interpreter's viewpoint usually defines its essence.

The main problem, however, with this approach to political obligation is not the dubious possibility of just determining what tradition says, although this is no modest difficulty. The greater problem, the decisive one, is that there is no particular reason to assume that just because something has been done in a certain way in the past, it *ought* to be done that way in the future. Why does it follow that because your father served in the military you are obligated to do so? What is there that is specifically *moral* about the past? It may be moral or it may not be. So with customary understandings of one's political duties and obliga-

[3]E. Burke, *Reflections on the Revolution in France* (Indianapolis; Liberal Arts Press, 1955).
[4]M. Oakeshott, *Rationalism and Politics* (New York; Basic Books, 1962).

tions; they may be ethical or they may not be, but their antiquity decides nothing.

This point does not imply that we cannot learn a good deal from the past, from the mistakes as well as the insights of those who have gone before us, but it is something else altogether to believe that this is a moral grounding for political obligation. If a given set of acts of obligation or disobligation is morally substantiable, it should have its moral case presented and evaluated instead of advanced as acceptable or contemptible simply because it is traditional.

The pragmatic case for obedience exemplifies this point by trying to demonstrate that the past is good not merely because it is there but because it contributes to stability and a just society.

Consent

In our age and in our nation, neither natural or divine laws nor the appeal to the past have been the most familiar and characteristic style of political obligation argument, despite their continuing health. It is, instead, *consent* that is the usual approach—as it has been for a long time. American revolutionary times were filled with phrases such as "no taxation without representation" and "consent of the governed." Many revolutions since then have repeated the idea, rooted in the thought of John Locke in seventeenth-century Britain, that citizens owe political obligations to a state only so long as it is based on the will of its sovereign citizens, while stipulating that they may overthrow any political order when it fails to adhere to its solemn duty. Today, of course, virtually all governments in the world *claim* their foundations lie in popular consent and it is routine for governments, including ours, to invoke their alleged popular support as the justification for demanding that laws be obeyed and institutions honored. At the same time, revolutionary movements continue to invoke consent arguments, among others, to buttress their drive to remove regimes in power as the National Liberation Front in Vietnam or the rebels in the Portuguese colonies in Africa illustrate so well. Radicals with less revolutionary intentions, including many American black activists or draft-age Americans during the Vietnam war, also have maintained that they were excluded from the process of consent in America and therefore owed nothing to our political order. All of these pictures attest to the continuing vitality of considerations regarding consent in the councils of human thinking.

The contemporary tendency to attempt to settle political obligation disputes by invoking the magic concept of consent should not mislead us into the hopeful belief that consent is a simple notion, uniformly interpreted and applied. The truth is, perhaps, exactly the opposite, and the popularity of appeals to consent doctrine derives to a large extent from the fact that consent has meant so many contrasting things to thinkers and has had equally varying implications in concrete crises of political obligation. The widespread disagreement over what "consent" means, or what the extent of the responsibilities of a "consenting" person is, darkens the skies over every discussion of consent and political obligation. Consequently, many of the most intense disputes about political obligation today *accept* the idea that consent is the only proper theory of political obligation, but strongly *disagree* over the meaning of consent, especially as it applies to their concrete situation. In our age, this division has appeared when militant blacks or students have sometimes broken laws under a rationale that denied they had ever consented to the American system only to be faced with another perspective in the courts. There they were told in effect that such actions were unacceptable exactly because they were obligated citizens who had indeed rendered consent. Our first practical and intellectual problem with a consent-based theory of obligation, then, is to determine a good answer to the question of the *meaning* of consent.

It is already obvious to us that there are many possible answers, but the most obvious definition of consent is *direct consent,* the idea that a person is politically obligated only if he has taken a formal, legal, and public oath of allegiance to a given political system. It is evident that few people in the world are called on to make such an oath, but it is equally evident that it would be easy in most nations to meet the standards of direct consent. All a country would need is a regularized process for citizens to take oaths of consent periodically, perhaps at local post offices. Loyalty oaths of varying descriptions now exist for inductees into the U.S. armed forces, many teachers and for elected public officials, among others, and they cause little or no comment or challenge.

The real problem with the direct consent test is not so much whether it now exists, or could be easily made available, as it is whether its inherent *directness* disqualifies it as a justifiable act leading to political commitment. Signing a statement or declaring an oath is too formalistic and too insubstantial an action in terms of the lives of most of us to carry the enormous *consequences* that political obligation may require, including military service. Deep and abiding consent can scarcely be measured except by intense action or long term choice, neither of which most conceivable forms of direct consent promote. It is quite plausible, as has often been the case with loyalty oaths, that citizens would go through the motions of "consenting" as routinely as they apply for their new license plates—and with as little implied commitment. Probably few citizens would have to be coerced in most situations to give *direct* consent, but few also would probably believe they had given much of anything.

The resulting paradox is simply that, though direct consent *appears* to be the sturdiest and most moral form of political obligation, it is actually one of the worst. This paradox has long been perceived by political thinkers, few of whom agreed with Senator McCarthy and his allies in the 1950s that loyalty oaths would measure loyalty or expose Communists.

Most consent advocates advance the more considered view that genuine consent is best demonstrated by residence or by political participation—or at least the opportunity to participate. Their notions of consent may be termed *tacit* or *indirect* consent. These thinkers argue that selected measures of tacit consent, while less immediate than *direct* consent, actually are much more *substantial* indicators of consent. As we will see, their critics are suspicious, contending that proponents of tacit consent are more concerned to establish a moral basis for claiming people are obligated and must obey than they are to defend the moral right of individual choice (consent).

A famous theorist of tacit consent was the seventeenth century Englishman, John Locke, who maintained it was perfectly proper to believe that a person was politically obligated if he had lived in a country, travelled its highways or perhaps inherited property under its laws.[5] This classic view suggested that residence implied consent, assuming it was possible to leave. Many countries including our own more or less consciously employ this standard of consent, but it seems as empty in its own peculiar manner as is direct consent. Even if consent is to be indirect, mere residence scarcely suggests anything definite as a token of consent, unless the word consent carries no meaning of active, aware choice. Certainly some people proudly proclaim that their residence in a country is the proof of their chosen loyalty to it and of their willingness to bear political obligation in its cause, but there is little doubt that for many others residence is an accident of birth or circumstance more than a choice, while emigration represents an unrealistic alternative by any measure. The trouble with "Love It or Leave It" bumper stickers is that a great many people fall into neither camp.

Participation tests do compensate for this weakness by insisting that there must be *actions* in order for there to be consent and thus obligation. Yet if we use measures of political participation in the United States, we must reach the conclusion that most Americans are not obligated. If we took the most widespread category of political activity, voting in presidential elections, about forty percent of the adult population would seem to be nonconsenting, despite the fact that there is no other credible basis for concluding that this is a reasonable assertion. Matters are complicated by the fact that voting for president once every four years hardly seems to constitute a measure of consent with any more depth or length of intensity than direct consent demonstrates. Yet it is well established in political science that only less than ten percent of the population participates in politics in a more active manner than casting an occasional vote or two. But the crucial fact is that these realities do not appear to affect, much less undermine, the ordinary American's sense of political obligation, and the inability of the political participation test to tap this sentiment amounts to a fatal flaw.

Another form of the participation test marks the opportunity to participate politically as the appropriate requirement for political obligation. If a citizen has

[5]John Locke, *Two Treatises on Government* (New York; Hafner, 1948).

a roughly equal chance with his fellow citizens to affect the policies of his government, whether or not he chooses to exercise that right, then surely he should be obligated to support the political order he lives in. This test insists that the citizen must understand that political obligation will be the consequence of opportunity, and its advocates never fail to note that few societies, including our own, approach the goal of roughly equal opportunity. But the objective is possible, especially as public financing of campaigns is adopted. The test also mandates that a realistic opportunity for citizens to leave a country be made available in order for there to be any valid choice and laws such as those that forbade draft-age American men to emigrate during the Vietnam war must be abolished.[6]

A more serious consideration than the various practical problems that presently stand in the way of adoption of a participation test for political obligation is the bind in which minorities, especially consistently losing minorities, may find themselves in a political system where consent and obligation are tied to opportunity for political participation. Even if minorities have the *right* to participate (and do so), they could find themselves obligated to their own oppression, though not to the extent of the loss of their political rights. Depending on the nature of the minority, they might, for example, get no policy benefits, while being heavily taxed or they might have a set of social discrimination laws passed against them, as has sometimes been true of American blacks. While they might emigrate, this change of life is never easy, nor is it clear why they should have to leave more than anyone else. They were born and have made their lives here, too.

Many thinkers accuse the proponents of consent via the test of political participation opportunities of promoting a theory devoted more to order than to justice. The theory seems to insist that disadvantaged minorities are obligated no matter what unless they emigrate, leaving little room for civil disobedience or other tactics that might be followed by the citizen who rejects his political obligation while loving his country or his home. The critics say that the opportunity test like all the other tacit or indirect tests shows that its true interest is in getting obedience rather than respecting the individual (or group). This criticism motivates one last variety of consent, which concludes that most types of consent-based theories of political obligation are ill-concealed maneuvers to pry out of people a moral commitment without much genuine consent. This form, advanced by Professor Hannah Pitkin of the University of California at Berkeley, might be termed the deserved test, because it argues that one is obligated to a government only when its forms *and* its policies hypothetically would merit or deserve consent if the citizen were asked about them. The test tries to provide as

---

[6]A few years ago one of the authors tried to defend this view. See R.B. Fowler, "Political Obligation and The Draft" in D. Hanson and R.B. Fowler, Editors, *Obligation and Dissent* (Boston: Little, Brown and Company, 1971).

much meaningful consent as possible by substituting for direct or indirect consent an ongoing nonformal process of individual judgment or choice about one's government. Its enthusiasts insist that only it can honestly legitimate obligation because only it provides a living process of human choice.

The Pitkin view also raises a vital question explored by too few other variants of consent theory. It contends that what is at issue is not only evidence of consent, but also what should be consented to. While individuals may disagree about what governments or policies merit consent, Pitkin's point is that this aspect of consent is significant. Can it ever be legitimate to consent to one's enslavement? Can one ever consent to a political system in which one is part of a consistently losing minority? These queries highlight the suggestion that consent may be structured by government actions as well as individual choices.[7]

Yet the problems with this attractive theory are many. For example, the deserved theory makes too much of conscious judgment and overrationalizes human behavior; it would likely have the practical effect of ensuring the obligation of less educated and/or less aware people. It also leaves too much to *present* individual choice, allowing the individual to decide by his own standards whether a government is satisfactory with no attention either to community judgments or inclinations or to past decisions. The individual may not be right by "objective" criteria, but he alone must decide for himself. The evaluation of an individual's moral correctness in his act of obligation is either left to outside observers who care to evaluate such things for their own reasons or is left to the interplay of citizens and their ideas within a polity. This is so true that the skeptic of the Pitkin test can only wonder if it is about political obligation or the virtual avoidance of it in normal circumstances. Somewhere between the tacit consent theories, which are so concerned to justify political obligation that they eliminate consent, and ones that are so concerned about consent that they offer governments little chance to obtain morally sanctioned obedience except when there are no costs to the citizen, there must be a better solution within the popular framework of consent theory. Yet it has not appeared amidst the myriad contenders for that honor.

Group Theory

A somewhat more subtle obligation theory than consent is the group conept, which derives political obligation from group memberships or interactions. The proponents contend that one group or another is the center of every person's moral universe, structuring all obligations and consequently determining our political duties. Several examples illustrate the range that group conceptions

[7]H. Pitkin, "Obligation and Consent-II," *The American Political Science Review*, March, 1966.

cover. Some radicals have argued that their activity within their movement or party creates a group loyalty requiring them to arrange their broader political duties totally in line with their party's dictates. Some democratic thinkers have insisted that a citizen's activity in a *vibrant, participatory,* and *community-oriented* political order is the only legitimate basis for political obligation, regardless of murky debates over consent. Other writers have contended that so-called natural solidarities, groups to which one belongs by birth rather than choice, such as "humanity" or a class or race, constitute the proper ground for all obligations, including political commitments.

The Party As Group.   Lenin's famous revolutionary pamphlet, "What Is To Be Done" (1902), is justly renowned for its explicit and detailed theory of the action-oriented revolutionary socialist party, but it is also fascinating for its implicit and indirect conception of obligation in a political world. It is an apt example of the view that obligation in politics is built on an intense, intimate set of interactions among members of a group where members give everything to their cause and each other. This gift of commitment determines all else in their lives, including their stance toward the larger political order around them. The members' intense contact with their fellows, their sharing, creates moral solidarity. They share a cause in a life of struggle and service for that objective and it binds them in a web of obligation that is utterly impelling, from which no one may resign at whim. They may or they may not owe obligation to their state, but this is never a primary moral responsibility, always a matter of tactics, never decided by individual choice and never really of substantial importance. The party is first, indeed, the party is everything.[8]

An impressive—or frightening—example of this version of group obligation may be seen in Bertolt Brecht's play, *The Measures Taken* (1930), in which the "Young Comrade" is killed by his associates, the "Four Agitators," because he would not surrender his moral individuality to the dictates of his group, in this case, the Communist party. It defined obligation for its individual members. It admonished its members: "Do not see with your own eyes!" for "all of you are nameless and motherless, blank pages on which the revolution writes its instructions."[9]

Such a notion of group obligation is unattractive for a number of weighty reasons, but it is its exclusiveness that makes the least sense by either normative or empirical analysis. A view that defines the moral world of the committed, as the Russian anarchist Nechayev did in 1868 in his *Catechism of the Revolutionist,* as one in which the dedicated "has no personal interest, no affairs,

[8]V.I. Lenin, *What is to Be Done?* (New York; International Publishers, 1929).
[9]B. Brecht, *The Measures Taken in The Jewish Wife and Other Short Plays* (New York; Grove Press, 1965), pp. 100 and 81–82.

sentiments, attachments, property. . . . Everything in him is absorbed by one exclusive interest, one thought, one passion"[10] hardly respects the myriad moral duties that most people reasonably want to and do assume. People choose to have multiple obligations, with their political order as well as to friends, family, or more than one organization, for a variety of explanations, no doubt, but they do make the choice for a complex moral world time and again. Nor is there any moral basis for denying them such a decision or series of decisions in a long life. We assume, people assume, choice and responsibility as part of their rhythm of existence, whatever their views on rarified topics like free will or the reality of existential choices.

The fact that fanatics of a party reject multiple obligations is unfortunate enough, but it is seriously compounded by their impatience with the great Western ideal of the freely choosing individual. He is despised by the enthusiasts of obligation through party membership. Freedom of choice is the enemy, the freely choosing person is like the "Young Comrade," dangerous and confused, and he must be destroyed. At its extreme, this view of obligation eliminates the setting in which the problem of obligation arises, the conflict between the individual and the group. Eliminating the setting means eliminating the freely choosing person and with it the Western conception of individual dignity.

The Group as a Participatory Community.   A more common version of the group basis for political obligation wants to think about the general political order as a group and to suggest that when that order is composed of a community of participating citizens who are about equal in political power, they owe each other a political loyalty that is ethical in implication. This is the treasured objective of participatory democrats in all ages from Rousseau to the American New Left of the late 1960s. The hope is that such a society will be equal enough in its social and economic features so that political equality will be more than the rhetorical phrase it usually is. Their trust is that people, confident of their relative equality, will actively work together molding a practical as well as caring community. Their aspiration is a political order in which power will be sharply decentralized to small local units of government, since only there could community have a fighting chance to flourish and endure.

Sympathetic contemporary theorists of this ideal state of affairs, such as Michael Walzer, insist that while a person must choose to live in this order, it is not his *consent* to do so which is the basis of his political obligation so much as his activity with others in the best political order, in a living participatory political order. Thus, though he calls this a form of consent theory, according to our conceptual framework, it falls under this category because of the emphasis

[10]M. Nomad, *Apostles of Revolution* (New York; Collier Books, 1961); pp. 214–256 provide the quotation in the context of the entire story of the remarkable Nechayev.

on living the order, not merely consenting to it. Participation, then, goes far beyond mere consent. Walzer and other advocates of a genuinely participatory polity recognize the obvious reality that there are few, if any, contemporary societies that embody their norm and they repeatedly criticize the modern state for its remote and elitist nature.

Frequently, their conclusion is that in this age, groups in which one's participation is more direct and central to one's life, such as the family, necessarily carry greater moral weight than any supposed political obligation to a distant and irrelevant state. For them, for now, "the obligation to disobey" the state whenever it conflicts with more primary ethical commitments is the greatest lesson to be learned about political obligation, but their dream remains that the day will come when the political community will manifest their ideal and become the primary group worthy of abiding obligation.[11]

There is much to be said for the viewpoint of participatory democrats because they recognize the individual as well as the group, because they demand that the group must be of its members and because they accept a universe of many obligations. But they seem unable to explain what is the central, vexing aspect of a group basis for political obligation: why participation creates (political) obligation. Why do citizens owe each other obedience if they have participated together in a political order? For example, why should we believe that participation ever has mattered much to the great bulk of humankind, who have rarely shown much interest in politics but often are ready to make arrangements for the benefit of themselves, their families, or their country? Perhaps people often have wanted to have a say about their fate, but even more they seem to have sought to have lives they defined as good and they have not always seen the two concerns as the same. The participatory democrats' ideal falters because it is an ideal without many believers—today, in the past, or in the imaginable future.

The response of participatory democrats to this type of argument is always part incomprehension and part anger. They do not understand how such a pragmatic approach has anything to do with moral questions, and it is not clear they are wrong, even as they angrily point out that acquiescence in the world of the second best is a denial of human possibilities and ideals and a profoundly conservative stance.

The Group as a "Natural" Solidarity.   One last example of a group-derived ground for political obligation focuses on natural groups or solidarities. Marxists sometimes talk of the proletariat in a language that implies that the working classes have a moral commitment to each other that history has imposed on them because they are members of the proletariat class (group). Some blacks and some whites contend that racial categories ought to, and do, determine the

---

[11]Michael Walzer, *Obligations* (Cambridge, Mass.: Harvard University Press, 1970).

contours of obligation in a natural and irrevocable sense, as much current rhetoric of racial solidarity suggests. A broader appeal, and a much more creditable one, has been made to the humanity that all persons share in common. This approach seeks to persuade us that the natural similarity that we all share as human persons creates an overpowering obligation that must guide us. The obligation of humanity derived from our necessary participation in the human species deductively defines the parameters of our immediate political commitments: only states that affirm in the reality of their life and policy the ethical demands of the greater natural obligation—equal respect for all human beings—deserve any political obedience or respect. The vision of the Nurenberg trials, that there are "crimes against humanity" that may never be committed no matter what statist loyalties one may have, is an example of this concept in recent political history. In this case, it defined a set of outer limits that the obligation to humanity required governments not to trangress. For some modern thinkers, the idea of a supreme obligation to humanity is less a boundary on human action or political obligation than an affirmation of what amounts to a new version of the religion of humanity. For example, Albert Camus, the French existentialist, argued in *The Plague* that the supreme responsibility of the human person was to all mankind and not any single state or political party. The human group mattered most of all, and the state was a distant entry on the list of ethical priorities.[12]

None of these solidarity arguments can carry many people with them unless the individual happens to respect the ethical content of "nature" that each theory normally proposes. Only a Marxist will agree that proletarian solidarity is natural and only those for whom humanity is defined more by its unities than by its manifold particularities can be an enthusiast for the supposed unity of humanity. Nature, indeed, has proved astonishingly capable of an infinitude of definitions and while this fact does not prove that one or another version might not be true, it is hard for those who are not already convinced to understand or to sympathize with that possibility. To believers this may only seem like perverse willfulness, but to the frequent skeptic in this unbelieving age it is a stance that sometimes will make sense. Yet there is surely something far more convincing for the skeptic about Camus' argument about our natural solidarity as people than about more transcendental natural laws, for we can at least see the people (if not always their solidarity!).

It is reasonable to wonder, in any case, why the "natural" group basis for obligation should be so appealing to many sensitive people if they honor the individual person as well. Natural obligations are not of our own volition, and indeed they deny any moral role to the individual. In this way, as in many others, they appear to be modern versions of natural law. Few proletarians, if any, in the

---

[12]A. Camus, *The Plague* (New York: Alfred A. Knopf, 1948).

Marxian scheme can choose to escape their class, few blacks can pass as whites and none of us can choose membership in another species. The unpleasant truth is that so-called natural obligations, even the lofty obligation to humanity, represent faith rather than freedom, a strange position for Western thinkers who, for so long, treasured moral choice and personality and placed them at the core of their moral faith.

Only a thinker with the extraordinary moral sensitivity of an Albert Camus is able to walk the tightrope that acknowledges that the individual must continue to *choose* while at the same time cites the natural obligations of humanity, such as equality. For Camus no natural obligation can achieve its fullest moral worth unless the ethical person accepts it, but too many other enthusiasts of the natural solidarity approach see it as an end to human choice, which is not at all Camus' wish.

Benefit Theory

A fifth and final disposition toward obligation concerns itself strictly with benefits. It looks at obligation as a payment that a citizen makes in return for what he obtains from membership in a political order or from following the laws of a particular government. Obedience or resistance ultimately flow from the answer to the old pragmatic question of "What have you done for me lately?" This is a response to problems of obligation that is a common one underlying the enthusiasm many Americans have felt for their political order, although it is also the practical basis for the conviction of many Americans who are black that they owe little to our political system.

This disposition is quite close in some features to consent tests that use political or economic participation as their evidence for consent, since they claim, in effect, that the receipt of selected gains (political or economic) from government means consent and thus mandates obligation. Yet it differs from consent criteria that depend on participation because it dispenses with all the elaborate philosophical baggage of consent theory. It simply says that if I am gaining from the order, I owe it something (obedience) in return, whereas I owe it nothing if I am not gaining from it.

In general, benefit theories do appeal to us more than any other so long as they require that any definitions of benefit be both socially concerned and based on agreed standards. Critics doubt if it is possible for societies to unite on general standards of benefits, but there is no reason to assume that this is an impossible task. People may well be able to agree on a series of services and rights that could make up a minimum definition of what a citizen ought to expect from his political order. Nor should the advantage of a benefit theory be ignored in so far as it places governments on notice that they exist not by divine or natural right, not because of some dubious, stretched, hard-to-measure "consent" but because they are to assist citizens. Regimes should meet tests for us, for our benefit, and, when they do not, there is no reason for us to feel or to owe obligation to them. No one, nor any people as a whole, should be embarrassed to ask of his government the question "What have you done for me?" No elaborate philosophical structure concerning consent theory or anything else should drive us from this instrumental view of politics. If a government helps a people by the people's lights, they owe it their allegiance, if it does not, they owe it nothing——and indeed they ought to get rid of it.

It may be asked how this disposition accords with our definition of political obligation at the beginning of this chapter. We stated there that it is widely agreed that obligation is a matter of morality. Yet critics charge that the benefit approach cares only about personal gain. What they forget is that the idea that government exists for the benefit of its citizens is an ethical idea, one of the greatest moral ideals of all times. To base political obligation on benefit is to acknowledge the moral principle that government should be instituted for our needs and desires.

Others fear that a benefit theory of obligation will buttress anarchism, the view that one can never be legitimately obligated. At its worst, anarchism dismisses the need for a society to have political cohesion to some degree if it is to survive and approves the lopsided, selfish doctrine that it is right to get something (benefits) for nothing (no commitment to obey). The benefit theory, as we have developed it, does not even resemble the quasi-anarchical Pitkin concept of deserved consent, which leaves judgment up to the individual, because we insist that there must be general standards for a world in which we must live together in interpersonal relationships that are inescapable.

CONCLUSION

While a benefit theory of obligation makes the most sense to us, and we have defended its claims, the broader objectives of this chapter have been to give some clear idea of the alternative ways in which people have reflected about political obligation and the tremendous importance of their reflections. Because this is not a simple matter, but rather a challenging one, it is natural sometimes to pretend we can escape it. Some undertake to do so by asserting that there is no *practical* need to worry about how to answer the summons of obedience or disobedience. Most people get along with their government—and most governments with their citizens—if for no other reason than the fact that the weight of every nation's socialization process is brought to bear on the task of insuring that its citizenry will be obedient, tractable men and women. Simple convenience works toward the same end. It is easy to obey and not think about it.

Sometimes this makes sense to us, because by such an approach one *avoids* the police and related problems, but the more common explanation is that many laws are obviously in our self-interest so, of course, most everyone would obey. Wearing a motorcycle helmet is easier than being stopped for not having one on, and it is usually conceded that it has concrete safety advantages too. Yet none of this has much to do with abstract phenomena such as political obligation and none of it constitutes much of an argument for not becoming interested in political obligation.

Similarly, the skeptic notes not only that the question of obedience is rarely a major anxiety for an individual or his nation, but also that when people do refuse to follow their government or its rules, the explanation rarely has much to do with theories of obligation. The suspicion once again is that mundane, "ordinary" motivations generate disobedience. People go through stop signs, for instance, when they find it necessary in practical terms (as when a mother in childbirth is being rushed to a hospital), or when they feel daring (as when teenagers are out on a Friday night), or when people inattentively do not bother to stop (as when people allow driving to take second place to their conversation or date).

However true or false these practical points are, for the person who is concerned with living a decent, ethical life, the catch to them is that the question is not just how *do* people often act, but how *ought* people act. Exploring political obligation challenges us to think about how we *ought* to act toward our political system, it calls on us to think as ethical people. Moreover, the experience of recent years as in the past suggests that we never know when we will be impelled by circumstance, by temper or by conscience to have to answer in life as well as in theory the ancient questions: Am I obligated? Are we obligated? Should I obey? Should we obey?

SUGGESTIONS FOR SUPPLEMENTARY READING

Burke, Edmund, *Reflections on the Revolution in France* (Indianapolis: Library of Liberal Arts, 1955).
Camus, Albert, *The Rebel* (New York: Vintage Books, 1956).
Lenin, V.I., *What Is To Be Done?* (New York: International Publishers, 1929).
Locke, John, *The Second Treatise on Government,* many publications.
Pitkin, Hannah F. "Obligation and Consent-II, "*The American Political Science Review,* March, 1966.
Socrates (Plato), *The Apology* and *The Crito,* many publications.
Walzer, Michael, *Obligations* (Cambridge, Mass.: Harvard University Press, 1970).
Wolff, Robert Paul, *In Defense of Anarchism* (New York: Harper & Row, 1970).

Authority and Revolt

We are, as Aristotle observed, "political animals." We inherit our interdependence. And the benefits of social interactions that we experience draw us toward political communities in spite of the risks and inconveniences that they inevitably bring. We accept crowded conditions and submit to unpleasant restrictions of individual liberty in order to share in such benefits as the provision for the common welfare and increased opportunities for achievement that political communities provide. We need a balance between dependence and independence, consequently each of us has a significant stake in our social and political structures.

To be sure, we have a taste and a tolerance for remarkable variety in political and social arrangements. History bears witness to a range of political communities from tightly organized, tiny nomadic clans to loosely integrated superstates, from simple oral agreements to reams of regulations, from an oligarchy of a few elders to monolithic bureaus, and every conceivable variation in between. There are even those who advocate a single political community of mankind—a concept that seems less ridiculous than it once did because global communications are reality. This diversity of institutions is ample evidence of our search for a viable polity. For example, anarchists who reject

states as we know them, and statists who embrace them, may disagree about what a desirable political community is, but they agree that the necessity exists to relate to each other, to accommodate our differences and to make the most of our potentials. The dispute between them and most of us centers not on the end but on the means—on how complex or simple, arbitrary, or permissive the community's institutions should be. Similarly, those who rely on divine guidance and those who do not agree on at least one point, the desire for political organization is a human characteristic. They may contend about origins and purposes, but there is consensus on the need for human beings to have polities.

If we accept states and their institutions as being permanent human phenomena, then questions about authority and revolt become important. In the twentieth-century the locus of politics is the nation-state in the overwhelming majority of instances. But wherever the locus we must establish a polity that furthers our aspirations and permits us to move beyond the bare rudiments of individual survival. Authority and revolt become significant factors in the establishment of desirable political communities. Even the most desirable political relationships lack permanence. And often our best efforts achieve something far less than the political ideal. We place great value on our polities because we need them. When they satisfy our desires and needs, we become complacent and bask in our good fortune. We do not foresee the need for prudent evaluation. But when states go awry we feel a keen sense of shock and emptiness and a suddenly urgent need to find viable alternatives.

LOYALISTS AND REBELS

Political institutions that mock justice and that pervert moral values are far from rare. Even the most casual student of history knows about the terrors of Stalinist dictatorship, the horror and depravity of The Third Reich, the chilling stories that filter out of the "Banana Republic" military juntas and other instances of the suffering and enslavement that people experience too often regardless of time or place. Even in the United States the extremely poor, the rural and ghetto black, sometimes feel the arbitrary baton of the angry police officer and experience deprivation of civil liberties or incarceration resulting from the inadequacies of a system that forces people to languish in frightful institutions like the "Tombs" prison in New York City. We may be shocked to discover that the government we have come to depend on and believe in has, in some instances, changed from one of protection to one of persecution. Even if we are not affected personally, we can see less fortunate citizens denied the benefits of freedom and justice.

When polities perverts justice not only do the directly affected victims suffer, but also those who have come to view political institutions as being truly public spirited become disillusioned and no longer have a polity that can be depended on. We do not want chaos and unfulfilled opportunities and the disappearance of formerly dependable stability is chaotic and unfulfilling. This is why we approach questions about the relative merits of our state and the possibility of revolt with great reluctance, if at all. Yet, we must question our politics. To face an issue suddenly and without preparation is far worse than to face it armed with the knowledge and understanding that only comes from careful political thinking.

There is, in our literature, a large body of ideas that examines the abuse of authority, injustice, and revolts that they cause. Revolt is inextricably a part of the political relationships within a state, the denial of justice, the abuse of authority, and individual and collective political obligations. Before an individual elects to seek redress through rebellion or to accept conditions complacently, he should decide whether the state has legitimate authority and therefore deserves his obedience and loyalty, or whether the state has abused authority entrusted to it. If a polity is legitimate—that is, if its authority does not stem from a tyrannical abuse of power and serves moral ends—individual decision may not be difficult. However, if the polity is only partially representative, or if it is wholly tyrannical, the individual is confronted with a difficult task. He must construct a thoughtful base for action, built on judgment and argument about fundamental questions of political morality.

The misuse of authority and the rebellion it creates is common and affects individuals and governments regardless of time or place. In the comparatively short history of the United States, its citizens have had to choose between loyalty to England and armed opposition, between following Daniel Shays in his armed rebellion against the government and accepting unfulfilled promises to the common farmers, between slavery and freedom for blacks, between Northern and Southern forces in the Civil War, between support for American involvement in the war with Mexico and the disobedience Thoreau encouraged, between gunboat diplomacy by which we seized the Panama Canal and opposition to unlawful acquisition, and between support for territorial expansion in the seizure of the Philippines and peaceful coexistence with China, among other issues.

Nor has our own era escaped crises of authority and rebellion. The Vietnam war and the opposition and resistance to governmental regulation that it prompted is a recent example. There are, even now, Americans in foreign countries whose protest of the Vietnam war led to their exile and who have not lessened their adamant rejection of American policies and authority. The headlines report the rebellion of those who oppose compulsory busing by using peaceful civil disobedience and sometimes violence. The Amish who object to compulsory public education on religious grounds wage a continuing battle with public school officials in several states. Many blacks in the United States feel that they have been the victims of discrimination for centuries and that they owe nothing to the country that perpetuated the inequalities. Ghetto riots in the 1960s appeared sometimes to be open, if inchoate, rebellion.

The members of the Committee to reelect the President who were in the Watergate scandals admitted that many acts Richard Nixon ordered them to perform were illegal or immoral. Were their actions justified on the grounds of national security? Were they morally committed to continue to be loyal to the authority which originally justified their acts or to rebel against it? Daniel Ellsberg, the defense analyst who originally supported American Vietnam war policy but changed after seeing classified documents detailing our policies and tactics, was placed in a similar dilemma. Was he obligated to continue to support the authority he had sworn loyalty to? Was his decision to disassociate himself from that authority justified? Should he have given those documents to *The New York Times?* Should the *Times* and the *Washington Post* have rebelled against the authority of the state by printing what Ellsberg had given them? People who opposed the Vietnam war but nevertheless were asked to serve in the military forces in Vietnam or required to pay taxes to finance the war were forced to make a choice. What should they have done? Those who are asked to make substantial economic or personal sacrifices in an alleged energy crisis while they read daily headlines about the lack of sacrifices and record profits of energy companies are also faced with choices. What should they do?

No matter what our position in the polity, as these examples show, each of us is liable to be faced with hard choices about authority and revolt. The examples here are American, but the problems are universal. If we are confronted by situations that run counter to our morality, we should at least consider whether we ought to continue our former obligations in spite of changed circumstances or whether we should (or must) seek to oppose injustice through revolt. The price of political interdependence, the continuing application of moral evaluations, cannot be avoided if we want to live in political communities which benefit citizens instead of leaders.

The Moral Dimensions of Revolt

The moral dimensions of authority and revolt demand a careful analysis because they are an integral part of responsible citizenship. This analysis is based on our theories of political obligation and the values that support them. In fact, the whole process of thinking about authority and revolt can best be viewed as a logical progression from understanding of political obligation to prescriptions about the ends and means of revolt.

Like all political theory, obligation begins from a basic political value. Usually this value is some variation on the theme of the sanctity of life (although any other value is possible). Therefore, in most familiar obligation theories, whether the stress is placed on the individual as in the liberal tradition or the collectivity as in the socialist or anarchist traditions, the claim is advanced that political communities should exist to secure conditions that are favorable to life. Other norms often valued and defended include liberty, equality, justice, and participation. It is just a step down the road to the position that we ought to be obligated to each other within and through political communities that make such values secure.

A theory of political obligation is a sword with two sharp edges. In the delineation of a set of values and policies embodied in a good polity, an obligation theory functions as a standard by which to measure the appropriateness of our loyalty to that polity. For example, if our theory of obligation justifies obligation only to a state that maximizes the general welfare of the community while it protects specified individual rights of each citizen, we have a clear definition of the aims of a legitimate political authority. If we then apply this concept to a particular state and find that the polity in question fails to measure up to its obligation to its citizens, are we obligated to it? Of course not. Its claims on our loyalties depend on its discharge of obligation. Our specifications of what is right tell us that this particular political community is immoral. In addition, it gives us a set of standards to determine how immoral it is—we can compare the distance between specifications and performance and thereby determine the seriousness of the situation. Continuation of even our once-justified political obligation in this circumstance would mock our values and commit us to immorality. Thus, our theory of what is right (the first edge of the sword) also tells us which states we are morally obligated to support and which ones we should not follow (the second edge) as well as giving us a measure of relative state immoralities. We must use both of these edges in cutting through the thicket of questions of authority and revolt in order to reach a morally defensible position. When we put our values to work in this way, we discover the degree of legitimacy in our political communities and open up to view a great many alternatives of justifiable citizen behavior.

Although the process of political thinking described here appears to be simple and perfectly rational, the application of the process is often quite complex. For one thing, political systems cannot be neatly segregated into absolutes of black and white, good and evil. We often have difficulty in identifying many of the factors that we must consider for the assessment of a complex political community. Even when we are able to identify general trends and much specific detail, our assessment depends on how our values fare in the present, how they have evolved historically and their most likely survival in the future. There is no available guaranteed formula to apply. Critical judgment must be exercised in such important determinations and that requires understanding, reflection, and rational evaluation.

But, we all know, the times when the calm voice of reason is needed most are often those when it eludes us. Tyranny and social upheaval carry us to the brink and often over the precipice of crisis, clouding dispassionate and reasonable assessment of events, inflaming emotions, arousing our narrow self-interest, and blinding us to the possible conflict of our acts with our ultimate values. Thucydides, for example, was deeply involved in Athenian policy making during the time when the critical decisions to enter the Peloponnesian war were being made;[1] his position on the question of whether Athenian imperialism was wrong and whether to maintain his loyalties to her after a long exile and disgrace was surely influenced by his particular, personal interests in the situation. Perhaps he might have looked at things differently were he an ordinary citizen. Or, consider the case of Sir Thomas More who had to choose between his obligations to his king and his church on the question of sanctioning a royal divorce.[2] Was his refusal to obey royal orders, emanating from a monarch who was likely to get his way in any event, worth More's head? In this case, revolt can certainly be judged to have been futile though not obviously foolish. Yet, More's devotion to the church and his stubbornness in time of crisis did not allow him to make a rational assessment; he never seriously considered any path other than one to the executioner.

Yet, even when we find it difficult to follow a reasoned progression from basic political values to decisions about revolt, we must try to do so. We cannot eschew this reasoned progression if we want to maintain polities that enhance the prospects of a just public accommodation instead of an uneasy coexistence built on mutual suspicion. Turbulent times above all others demand thoughtful ethical concern if we are to avoid nihilism and irrationalism when their lure is greatest.

We may not always succeed but we must make the attempt if our political obligations and values are not to be merely hollow words recited at patriotic occasions.

Since political communities vary widely in their worth, our first task is to decide which deserve our political obligation and which do not. When we find that a given polity is one that is consistent with our values and, therefore, is in our judgment, authoritative, we have only to determine an appropriate way to fulfill our obligations. But, when we cannot obligate ourselves to a particular polity because it conflicts with our values, we must find the most appropriate avenues of opposition to it in order to give meaning to our values.

In this latter instance, we face two critical questions; what levels of political opposition are required, and what means may we use to pursue them? The answers to these questions depend primarily on our personal values and the personal risks we are willing to take. These two questions are recurrent. No

[1]Thucydides, *The Pelopennesian War* (New York: Oxford University Press, 1960).
[2]Robert Bolt, *A Man For All Seasons* (New York: Random House, 1962).

citizen has complete immunity to issues of authority and revolt. An analysis of some of the more important political theories dealing with these issues can prepare us for the sudden or gradual advent of these issues into our personal world.

Provisional Obligation

Most citizens are satisfied, or at least not actively dissatisfied, with their states. This may only be due to their low levels of expectation that arise from past deprivations and the political socialization process in which family, schools, churches, peer groups, and the like often work in concert to reinforce satisfaction with public institutions (whether deserved or not) that at the same time encourage only limited involvement. Whatever the cause, even the most casual survey will show that in most polities, including our own, a majority of people are not actually dissatisfied with their institutions. However, even citizens who think carefully about their values and the role that states should be playing often obligate themselves to a particular political community.[3] After all, a good many states plod along doing a minimally satisfactory if unspectacular job of administration to many public needs. This presumes, of course, that these polities were conceived with some justice and that they are not led by uncharacteristically evil men who have blocked the reform process that allows policy to change with the times.

The citizen who lives in a state that is good or, as is often the case, one that he perceives to be good is fortunate because he faces no great moral crises. It is easy for him to accept his obligation when the state accomplishes what he values. His only real problem is to discover how to discharge his moral obligation in an appropriate way. Thus even though such a citizen need not actively concern himself with revolt, he must still ask himself what duties his obligation entails. Also, since his obligation is rooted in his values as well as the actual performance of the government itself, he must realize the inherently tenuous nature of obligation to a specific political community.

The question of what constitute morally appropriate modes of obligation has been answered by a great many political thinkers. Additionally, policy makers deluge us with what they feel are valid civic duties for obligated citizens. For example, a form of the "benefit theory" of obligation as advanced by many governments (including the United States) claims that we must serve in the military if drafted because we have benefitted from the advantages of citizenship and, therefore, we owe the state obligation—as determined exclusively by the state. We agree that the benefit theory of obligation is persuasive,[4] but the form in

---

[3]See Chapter 7 for a review of political obligation and Chapters 6 and 8 for discussions of the nature of authority and justice as they relate to political communities.
[4]See Chapter 7.

which this obligation to the state should be fulfilled must respond to the individual as well as the state. People often have multiple obligations, to ideals, families, or jobs, as well as to the state, obligations that by definition have moral weight. A state, like an individual, must acknowledge the complex moral debts and responsibilities most adults have, just as an individual who has benefitted from a state must not seek to escape his resultant obligation.

Some citizens refuse to participate in wars, for example, even if they have an obligation to the state, claiming they have a higher obligation to moral laws against war. Some governments, on the other hand, often ignore citizens' multiple obligations, including those some may have to moral laws against war, and demand that everyone actively support a war. Neither position is very convincing. The provision of alternative service represents a positive step that several modern societies, including our own, have taken to avoid such dilemmas in a real world in which people have multiple obligations. In this case, alternative service offers a way for citizens to acknowledge both their obligations to higher law and to the state.

We may well owe a good political community a great deal, but since a political community is good only insofar as it serves the interests of its members, its calls to duty must harmonize with the other obligations and values citizens have as much as is humanly possible. Polities can do much in this regard and perhaps we may reject a claim to duty to even the best of states if the only rationale for such a claim is official endorsement that rests on a limited view of the public interest.

If we look to the history of political theory for guidance, we see that the ancient Greeks delineated a group of civic responsibilities that remain sensible in our age.[5] They argued that the obligated citizen ought to participate in all of the civic decisions, duties, and opportunities that were permitted to him by the constitution and customs of his polity. He ought to be informed about the issues of the day, honor the best interests of his fellow citizens, and take advantage of the full rights of citizenship accruing to people in his particular polity.

The validity of such a view can best be illustrated by comparison with the prescriptions of the medieval theorist St. Augustine. He felt that temporal communities existed only as way stations before eternity. The sinful nature of unsaved individuals caused nations to be hotbeds of greed and depravity. They existed to save people from themselves and give them a chance at salvation. The civic duties owed such a polity include unquestioned obedience irrespective of individual citizens' values. The obligation was owed to God through the polity and if the state said to die for it, the good citizen must do so because God wills only justice in the long run.

---

[5]Thucydides, op. cit. See his sketch of Athenian citizenry and civic duty throughout his book, particularly when he is discussing Pericles.

Many theologians and political theorists from Aquinas to Niebuhr have rejected at least the political aspects of these claims. While not denying divine authority, they have claimed that the political community is a human one and consequently must be organized around human values and needs.

A modern adaptation of the classical Greek position is on the right track. Thus, one whose idea of a good polity has been fulfilled by his state owes to it behavior that will continue to make it good for him and for his fellow citizens. His civic participation will tend to keep the polity consistent with what caused it to become the accepted authority in the first place. Therefore, the polity cannot violate his political values.

While we may quibble with the specific application of the Greek theory, it does make sense that the fulfillment of the aspirations of its citizens is what makes a state authoritative. Citizens should do what is expected of them and exercise full legal rights, and advocate constitutional change as long as their values are not being violated by the state.

The test issue of political obligation often is when the state may ask citizens to give their lives. The seventeenth-century English thinker Hobbes and the eighteenth-century Swiss thinker Rousseau exemplify two classic opposing views on the obligation to die for the state as the ultimate civic duty.[6] Hobbes felt that the state ought to exist only as an instrument designed to fulfill the right of self-preservation for each of its citizens. No one was ever obligated to die for it.[7] On the other hand, Rousseau thought that the polity was so much a beneficial aspect of the common life of its citizens that it was proper to expect a citizen to risk death for it so that the benefits of the political community would be preserved for others.[8]

While fairness to Rousseau demands that we point out that he meant this only for politics that were radically egalitarion and democratic (as in his *Social Contract*), the issue between Rousseau and Hobbes, apart from their particular formulations, remains a basic one. For those who view provisional obligation favorably, Hobbes' argument will seem most convincing. His insistence that the sanctity of life is a basic political value will not be discredited by any arguments for the organic unity of a political community or any other collectivist arguments that do not recognize the individually-based needs for a polity. To them no state can expect its members to violate their most cherished values (their right to existence) simply because it has provided them with other valued things such as good relationships with fellow citizens. The most positive benefits of a good public life are derivative from life's continuance for each and every citizen.

Advocates of provisional obligation insist that the duties owed to a good state

[6]Michael Walzer, *Obligations* (Cambridge, Mass.: Harvard University Press, 1970), pp. 77–98.
[7]Ibid, p. 87.
[8]Ibid.

are proportional to its inclusion of human values that are the basis of our theories of obligation. In the final analysis, we are obligated *to* other citizens *through* our political communities. Institutions are not thinking entities and cannot enter into moral relationships such as obligation. They are merely convenient vehicles through which individuals relate to each other. We permit the polity to be authoritative only insofar as it is governed by political values. This being the case, the wise citizen should view his obligatory civic duties to the beneficiary political community through a lens of constant moral reevaluation. Good states do go awry, and we should attempt to prevent that possibility by viewing the actions of even the best states in a mildly skeptical manner. To do otherwise is folly because an unconstitutional pledge of civic duty without a guarantee of our values is a mindless act of automatic obedience, not the thinking act of a sophisticated citizen. The surest way to guarantee the existence of authoritative political communities is to populate them with authoritative citizens who will ask hard questions about the benefits of every government.

Advantages of Provisional Obligation

Provisional obligation has much to offer many citizens. First of all, it is characterized by moral and rational behavior instead of merely reflexive acts usually associated with patriotism for its own sake. To be sure, political communities are valuable[9] and they should be given the benefit of the doubt on questions of authority. They ought not be disposed of on a whim or a momentary passion. Provisional obligation accomplishes these goals quite effectively. Provisional obligation presumes that a state that fulfills the valid moral objectives that constitute its being should be obeyed and asks only that the forms of civic duty associated with obedience be consistent with the moral rationale for the state. Moreover, in its requirement for constant reassessment provisional obligation gives clear criteria for the specific bases of a political community's authoritativeness. It places the heavy requirement of moral evaluation and active citizenship on the ordinary person, but it also gives fair value for the price exacted: it improves the prospects of good polity by providing direction for other actions when the polity is less than good. The entire idea of the social contract theory in Western history (in the political theories of Hobbes, Rousseau, Locke, Jefferson, and others) is intimately associated with such a view of provisional obligation. While the various social contract theorists do not agree on the exact nature and limits of the civic duties expected, their agreement on the notion that correct thought and behavior results in provisional obligation for the obligated citizen is impressive and sufficient cause for us to take this particular theory of authority and revolt seriously.

[9]See the discussion of the relationship of political institutions and the need for politics in Chapter 2.

Partial Obligation

When most of a polity's institutions, laws, and policies are morally valid and deserve obligation but some particular ones are not, the citizen is in a dilemma. He is morally obligated to those aspects of the community that are good. Hence, he cannot simply reject the polity and work for its overthrow. However, he should not tolerate its evil aspects either. In such a situation, he has no choice but to be simultaneously a loyal citizen and a sworn enemy of selected aspects of his political community—partially obligated and partially rebellious. He must be loyal to that which is morally valid. He must oppose and work to change that which is immoral—that which he cannot obey. His civic duty is to act loyally to the extent that the polity merits it and not to when it does not fulfill basic standards for political obligation.

The Question of Civil Disobedience

While people seek to change society to accord more adequately with their norms by many means, none is more controversial nor raises more important questions in political philosophy, except revolution, than acts of civil disobedience. Civil disobedience may be defined as any purposeful, public act of disobedience to any policy, institution, or law. It is usually employed by those who consider themselves partially obligated only after more conventional and legal means of change have been exhausted. It is particularly suited to the dilemma of the partially obligated. Practioners of civil disobedience follow this route rather than revolution because they seek to improve rather than overturn the society and do not deny that it is adequate in many other areas. To advocate revolution is to declare war on a political community and to deny its authority altogether.

Civil disobedience has several important characteristics. First, it is an act of what Walzer terms the "morally serious" citizen.[10] It is not the criminal act of a thief that is carried out in his own self-interest and has no valid claims of political morality associated with it. The civil disobedient acts in a public—a political —manner that is designed to educate his fellow citizens about a moral crisis. He tries to point out a wrong by his opposition and to cause people in and out of the policy process to become concerned enough to put a halt to the outrage. Far from doing something in his own interest and hoping to slink away and escape detection and punishment like a thief, a person acting on the basis of political morality commits an act in full public view with the clear intention of being caught and tried so that his prosecution can be viewed publicly as persecution and stand as an example of moral bankruptcy. He schedules his act so that it can be seen and understood by the largest audience and to ensure that he will be

[10]Walzer, op. cit., p. 20.

apprehended. Some even go so far as to alert the news media and the police beforehand. There is no private benefit in being arrested, incarcerated, and risking the prospect of severe punishment. No jewels are stolen, no banks robbed, and no fortunes made by civil disobedients. Their only victims are immoral policies.

Acts of civil disobedience have occurred frequently in American history. A few examples may illustrate the political and moral character of the act. Perhaps the most famous incident of civil disobedience in our history was the Boston Tea Party, in which a group of colonists threw a cargo of British tea overboard in Boston Harbor to protest the taxation the British had levied against Americans without giving them representation in the government that passed the levy. This was a classic example of accepting overall British authority (it was not an act of rebellion that was to come later) while protesting a specific policy.

It followed our definition in every way except that the participants tried to hide their identities to escape British wrath, although they communicated who they were in general and why they had acted by public notices. The moral significance of their act would have been enhanced if as a demonstration of the colonists' will to resist, they had allowed the British to capture them. Nevertheless, it was civil disobedience.

In recent years the conscientious resistance to the draft for military service was also civil disobedience. Many young men when called refused to take the oath of induction or publicly destroyed or returned their registration cards to protest conscription policies that they felt were immoral. Many willingly went to jail rather than to the army. Those who fled to Canada and other places rejected the whole polity and did not commit civil disobedience. But the ones who stayed refused and willingly took their punishments were operating entirely within the boundaries of civil disobedience. Similarly, the act of Daniel Ellsberg who made public classified documents detailing the nature of American foreign policy in Southeast Asia and the defiant willingness of the editorial staffs of *The New York Times* and the *Washington Post* (and later other newspapers) to print the material given to them by Ellsberg in order to protest the nature of American actions and to produce public outrage at these policies fall within the realm of civil disobedience as well. There have been countless other such acts by Americans in the past and present ranging from the antiwar efforts of various Quaker protestors to mass antibusing protests.

Conscientious law breakers affirm the authoritative nature of their political communities by their choice of civil disobedience rather than more sweeping protests such as revolution. They communicate the idea that the state has a right to have institutions and policies, to pass laws and to punish violators by their willingness to be caught and to accept punishment for their acts if their legal and political defenses failed. They demonstrate their political obligations by caring enough about public policies to be concerned about their effect on others. They believe that people need political communities to relate effectively to each other. They show a desire not to destroy the polity and a passion to improve it. Thus, any act that is really civil disobedience must be without intentional private gain, must be open, and must be clearly justified through communication of its moral rationale. Moreover, it must be limited. The aim is to improve the state by purging it of evil and, therefore, the disobedient eschews the moral outlook and the tactics of the revolutionary and of the totally obedient. He steers a careful middle ground of courageous moral seriousness butressed by political obligations.

Some thinkers like Hugo Bedeau have maintained that civil disobedience must be nonviolent in order to fall short of revolution.[11] Such claims are understandable because they focus on the inherently limited nature of civil disobedience. However, the absence or presence of violence is not relevant as a factor of definition for civil disobedience. Its absence or presence is not without a great deal of moral relevance, however. Such famous acts of civil disobedience as Captain John Brown's violent raid on Harper's Ferry in opposition to officially condoned slavery certainly qualify as civil disobedience. They were designed to change policies and to shock a nation into preventing further immorality. Yet the fact that they were violent is morally suspect, at least. It is impossible to avoid the moral contradiction of killing hundreds in order to free others from bondage. The ends may be laudable, but if the means used to get to them besmirched them, the civil disobedient is no better than those against whom he directs his acts.

There are several considerations regarding the issue of violence and civil disobedience that should be looked at because it is so important. First of all, one must be careful about the word violence. While it is normally understood as the use of force to injure or abuse, we must distinguish between violence directed at bricks, mortar, and wood (i.e., violence against property) and violence directed against people. There may be a great deal less suffering caused by violence against property than there is in violence employed toward people. The latter is usually more serious and more worthy of moral condemnation. An act of civil disobedience that encompasses violence should be as limited in that respect as possible and clearly likely to lower violence in the long run (such as violently destroying a barracks of storm troppers and thereby preventing them from killing tens of thousands) if it is to be defensible on moral grounds.

Second, it should be understood that practitioners of civil disobedience do not agree on the relative pragmatic merits of violence. Violence is often thought to be more effective, all other things being equal, because pacific sentiments are felt to "be in the way" and "petty moralisms" have no place in the tactics of

---

[11]See, for example, Hugo Bedeau in Donald Hanson and Robert Booth Fowler, *Obligation and Dissent* (Boston: Little, Brown and Company, 1971).

those who stand up courageously against injustice. This rationale for violent civil disobedience is of dubious merit. Careful planning and intelligence can make nonviolent actions tremendously effective. Violence is often the last resort of the incompetent. Those who feel that they ought to use it without any hesitation often are guilty of poor tactical vision.

We would point out that much of the violence in civil disobedience is preventable by better planning and intelligence and, in any case, tactical considerations should take a back seat to moral considerations in an act which is predicated on public morality. However, if some violence is necessary (as in the case of destroying the storm troopers), if something is to be prevented that would be much worse, the best principle is that of an economy of violence. The civil disobedient who wishes to give prominence to moral considerations should use the least violent tactics available to him and should reject any acts that would be extremely violent regardless of their intended consequences. There is a point, indeed, where what one does in the service of morality is so monstrous that it can never make up for what it would prevent. The civil disobedient must never reach that point and this is what gives at least partial credence to those who condemn violence in civil disobedience. Unavoidable violence in civil disobedience should be held to the absolute minimum. It is always regrettable and should never be celebrated.

Any evaluation of the moral appropriateness of civil disobedience has to take two major positions into account. The first one, held by such theorists as Bay and Thoreau,[12] claims that states will tend toward injustice unless they are curbed by justice-loving citizens. People who wish to see their political communities maintain morality therefore have a moral duty (to Thoreau) or a justifiable moral option (as Bay sees it) to renew public moral sensibilities by jolting public officials back to their senses. The claim is not that political institutions are evil and can do no good, but that large institutions tend to lose sight of their original goals of public protection and need occasional rude shocks to nudge them into regaining their original vision. Civil disobedience can supply such shocks. Both Bay and Thoreau claim in their own way that the civil disobedients should be viewed as the most loyal citizens because they are acting on their desires to see their polities live up to their promise and improve the quality of public life.

On the other hand, other thinkers like Augustine or Burke[13] opposed civil disobedience. They put a great deal more faith in the polity's intrinsic justice without assistance. Augustine believed that the state acts in concert with God's

[12]See Christian Bay, "Civil Disobedience: Prerequisite For Democracy in Mass Society" in David Spitz, Editor, *Political Theory and Social Change* (New York: Atherton, 1967); see also Henry D. Thoreau, *On The Duty of Civil Disobedience,* reproduced in scores of anthologies and volumes of his works.

[13]St. Augustine, *The City of God* in *St. Augustine: The Complete Works* (Edinburgh: Dodds, 1871–1876); or Edmund Burke, *Reflections on The Revolution in France* (Garden City: Dolphin, 1961).

plan and Burke held that it developed its policies and institutions through the arduous trials and errors of history and, therefore, was not likely to lose sight of its purposes or to serve injustice. Both suspected that any acts of disobedience were likely to be ill founded because public order is so fragile and they hoped that any seemingly unwise or unjust acts states might commit would be temporary. Civil disobedience, they claimed, might destroy the whole fabric of the community. They chose to hope that in time polities would be back on the right track. Thus, the risks of civil disobedience are not worth running. To tamper with what we dimly understand is to risk the unleashing of dark forces that may engulf us all before they are contained.

This latter position is not entirely implausible but it is greatly exaggerated and alarmist. On the other hand, many of our founding fathers would agree with Jefferson when he claimed that even the best conceived and administered of polities sometimes loses touch with the needs of its citizens due to the isolation of its leaders and the cultural lag intrinsic to institutions. It is not anarchic to reserve the right (some would take it even farther and make it a duty) to rerail our polities when they jump the track of justice. Augustine and Burke place too much faith in political institutions as they are. It is not realistic to expect them to stay on the track no matter what happens. We agree with them that states are valuable and should not be resisted on a whim, but we cannot concur in the claim that good reasons never exist for resistance or that limited resistance always leads to ruin. Reason may not require civil disobedience as often as Bay might like, but it certainly does not seem to prevent it.

States should be given the benefit of the doubt and opposed only when and insofar as necessary. The civil disobedient finds his state partially wrong and he feels justified in opposing it selectively in order to live his theory of obligation. It is quite true that no citizen must get involved and we cannot condemn those who do not or who hold other obligations to be prior. However, disinterest in politics and reluctance to embrace in civil disobedience when appropriate does nothing to improve things. There are times when a course of civil disobedience is in the long-range self-interest of those who seek the· best possible political communities, however distasteful it might be to the ordinary citizen who is unaccustomed to revolt. The short-run tactical risks and inconveniences that civil disobedience might cause should be balanced against the long-range gains it often accomplishes.

In trying to assess civil disobedience, we must conclude that it can often be a legitimate and justifiable response of those citizens whose theory of political obligation tells them to maintain their general political loyalties even when selected aspects of their polities are wrong and are beyond legal recourses of change. On a purely tactical level, civil disobedience will only succeed when the state and its citizens have at least a residue of moral concern. If you tried to lie down in front of Hitler's tanks in order to halt them, your act would be futile because it would be swiftly nullified by your being run over. Your deeds would go unrecorded and, therefore, would fail to stop evil. Nevertheless, purely tactical considerations should never take precedence in moral definition and analysis in political theory. Whether the tanks roll on to kill others or not cannot be blamed on you and cannot negate the heroism of your actions. An act of morally serious civil disobedience is a valid one regardless of whether its intended consequences are fulfilled or not. The citizen who feels his obligations command him to save the polity instead of rejecting it should consider civil disobedience as a valid alternative at his command.

States Without Authority: Ends, Means, and Morality in the Obligation to Disobey

There is a line, not always obvious, between authoritative and unauthoritative political communities. Those thinkers who judge their communities worthy of obligation obviously are dealing with a polity which is on the "good" side of that line. Civil disobedients, on the other hand, are frequently working with communities that straddle the line. There is surely a great deal of good in their communities or they would not feel that such polities are worth saving. However, some political communities are not morally justifiable. Such unauthoritative states have gone too far down the road to tyranny to be worthy of redemption. These are the kinds of polity that drive thinking citizens to revolution. A state that can put millions to death in concentration camps and bases its whole foreign policy on violent conquest, for example, should not be saved if one values life and its political implications. It should be overthrown and a more authoritative polity should be raised on its ruins.

The potential rebel has only his theory of obligation to guide him. He knows what legitimate authority is, he knows that he is not experiencing it. Beyond this, what is he to think? What issues will he have to consider? The first question is, why should he rebel? Which tactics ought he to embrace? The question of what justifies revolution will be analyzed at some length below. The second question is equally vexing and not easily answered.

First, however, we must ask why revolution is ever justified. We believe that no one need support an unjust state, but are there good grounds for actively opposing one? After all, revolution is a step fraught with serious moral and practical consequences. Almost all thinkers on revolution in the modern era agree that revolutionary opposition of one sort or another finds its legitimate justification in human "oppression" or "injustice." They also tend to agree that this step must always be a final, desperate action taken only when all other means of redress have been exhausted. They usually insist as well that oppression and injustice must be grievous and enduring in its impact. Revolutions must not be undertaken for light causes. They can cost too much in human life and suffering.

Where agreement ends, however, is over what constitutes "oppression" or "injustice" and over whom may determine when they exist. Thoreau is renowned for his declaration that it is up to every individual to decide for himself when government is doing great human evil and when he may revolt. Others have shared this anarchical notion, but it is a position that should not be lightly endorsed. There is always a reason to wonder if any individual, or even a minority group, can be so certain of its great grievances that they have a moral right to plunge a society into the dangers and destructions of revolution. Others warn that such individuals, if they are moved by genuine moral concern, must ask what good a society does for others, for the majority. Individuals should hesitate before they dismiss the benefits a society may provide others. If they exist, they cannot justify the oppression of individuals, but they do temper the case for revolution.

These considerations, among others, moved John Locke as well as many democrats to insist that a revolution cannot be legitimate unless a majority believes it is, unless a majority believes that the grievances and injustices in society are too great. They make majority opinion the definition of human oppression. They argue, as all democrats must, that government is properly founded in the consent of the governed. Only a majority may withdraw consent and justify a revolt. Otherwise, revolution may actually lead to a minority seizing power for its selfish interests in the name of its selfish notions of oppression.

A third common basis for revolution, which extends back to Locke also, but was used by American revolutionaries and has been cited by contemporary black leaders, insists that the test of human oppression must not be solely up to individuals or majorities, but recognized natural standards or rights. Violations of such alleged rights as the right to national self-determination, to political liberty, to equal political participation, or to equal fulfillment of basic human needs are often used as standards of oppression and injustice. The least controversial of them is the right to life itself. Certainly when citizens, whether a majority or a minority, find their very existence jeopardized by political institutions, it is hard to argue that they do not have a natural right to revolt. Of course, a society may decide it is necessary to proceed against these citizens anyway, but the point is that citizens may well have a right to resist actively. Hobbes went so far as to claim that a state that murders citizens is not a state at all, because governments exist in the first place to provide protection for their citizens.

Another frequently cited natural right that is alleged to justify modern revolutions is the "right" to national self-determination. Indeed, no rallying cry has spurred more revolutionary action in the past thirty years. Country after country has been born in Africa and Asia under the banner of the right to national self-determination. Even when independence took place before revolution, revolutionary forces were usually already at work, as in the former British colonies in Africa. Their invariable argument was that it was immoral for Britain, or France, or Portugal to deny indigenous peoples the right to govern themselves.

This cry is heard in the present day from the Palestinian guerillas and the rebels of Northern Ireland. It seems to be endlessly popular.

A fourth basis for revolt common in our age is that used by Marxist revolutionaries. They appeal neither to the individual, nor the majority, nor to one or another natural right. They use history, instead, as a justification for revolution. Marxists, including the revolutionaries of China and Cuba, argue that the historical process dictates when it is appropriate for men and women to revolt in order to realize history's destiny. They make history's supposed purposes into moral justifications of the highest order.

The problems with the selection of history as a basis of revolt are similar to those posed for natural rights. In both cases it is necessary to agree in the first place that history or nature contain discernible messages. History is so notoriously murky that it is read in many different ways by different people. How can we be sure that the Marxist readings are correct? Nature, and specifically natural rights, are a similarly fertile phenomenon. There are a great variety of conflicting opinions about which natural rights exist. How is anyone to know which are truly existent? Second, even if history does have a central direction, or contains certain rights, we must agree that their existence requires us to give them sound moral sanction before they can justify something as serious as revolt. Nature may well teach that life is a central value, but this does not necessarily mean that we *must* agree.

We conclude that there does not appear to be any simple formula that can tell us when revolution may be justified. There is here, as so often, no substitute for the process of normative argument and discussion in politics. We tend to think that revolution is best justified by majority sentiment. Justification by this standard is likely to avoid revolutions built on individual whims or historical fantasies. Yet we recognize that majorities can err and individuals will sometimes be morally right, whether they justify their revolt on the basis of their own judgment, history, or natural right.

Passive Revolt   Revolution or unlimited revolt is not the only form of complete opposition to an ongoing political regime. Intensity of opposition need not be measured by the degree of active belligerence directed toward any state. One general type of unlimited opposition to a state is passive. It does nothing overtly to oppose the institutions of the political community. The passive rebel does not throw bombs or act violently in opposition to an unjust state. Instead, he "merely" withdraws any form of loyalty and civic duty from the polity. He refuses to pay taxes, to obey laws and regulations, to be conscripted, and to do anything demanded of the citizen even if the demands might be legitimate in another context. Such a posture can be tremendously radical in its effect to which the general strikes in twentieth-century Europe will testify. No state can endure very long when its calls to duty are met with silence. No wars can be fought, no people exterminated, virtually nothing can be accomplished by a state that is passively opposed by enough of its citizenry.

There are several varieties of passive resistance. We have put them on a continuum of likely effectiveness. This is not to say that effectiveness may be equated with morality, but only that among morally equal positions, the one that will best prevent tyranny and injustice is preferable, because it has the effect of stopping immorality. The simplest passive resistance and most total is emigration, recently exemplified by the scores of thousands of non-Communist refugees from SouthVietnam. People who refuse a relationship with what they deem an unjust state often simply leave it and thereby weaken its grip on the populace by denying its authority and showing others that they should follow suit. While Hobbes condemned emigration and said it was an act of cowardice that he might understand and even condone in the right circumstances, but which he could never call moral behavior,[14] we only have to recall the many heroes like De Gaulle who have gone into exile and fought from outside their homeland to see that Hobbes overstated his case by a wide margin. For those who wish to emigrate and find circumstances favorable, it is often more effective to emigrate and keep a heavy stream of criticism and moral outrage trained on the fires of tyranny than it is to suffer in effective silence within the polity. In reality, though, emigration's effects are usually blunted because there are always enough people left behind who are willing to cooperate with, or unwilling to oppose, tyranny. Generally, emigration even by thousands of people affects polities that are more worthy of partial obligation that it does consumately evil ones because in immoral states, such acts are met with callousness or apathy. Emigration is not immoral and it can be moral and effective only if particularly talented people like the writer Solzhenitsyn can accomplish their opposition from exile or if more effective opposition can be organized only from abroad. Normally, however, emigration as an act of revolt is not so much immoral as futile.

For those who choose not to emigrate, one of the options is individual refusal to participate. This deliberate refusal of all civic duties differs from civil disobedience because it is not selective. Such a rebel does not support policies, refuses conscription, will not vote, and does nothing that will aid his polity. Unfortunately, because it is not done in solidarity with others, this, too, is often a quixotic path. Individuals acting alone cannot be effective against the might of the modern state even if their acts are morally justified. Moreover, the refusal to become involved with others similarly inclined is a desertion from the ideal of political community and human interdependence.

The most effective moral form of passive rebellion is collective refusal to participate as citizens. Through effective political organization, citizens who are

[14]Thomas Hobbes, *Leviathan* (New York: Crowell-Collier, 1962).

united in opposition can perform such overtly passive acts as blocking government services, general strikes,[16] the organization of counterinstitutions such as "people's hospital" run by citizens to care for victims of the state, and many other acts that do not explicitly attack the state but oppose it or show its bankruptcy.[15] Gandhi's campaign of nonviolent resistance to British occupation of India is the best example of collective passive resistance.

If well planned, collective passive resistance is powerful. The moral courage of those who would lie down unarmed in front of tanks and their refusal to kill in the name of justice can be a remarkable phenomenon. But it has its price too! The insistence on passive acts of opposition tends to put the rebels at a tactical disadvantage because they must react to the state's injustice and not strike preemptively. It requires a great deal of coordination, a great deal of patience and generally is the most difficult way to overthrow an evil state.

Its great advantage is that it rarely traps the rebel into unfortunate tactical contradictions of his or her basic values. For those pacifists whose theory of political obligation is firmly based on the sanctity of human life, it is the only permissible mode of revolution. Others who seek to avoid violence, while not absolutely ruling it out, also prefer at least to try passive resistence first. Like civil disobedience or provisional obligation, it can be both a moral and successful approach to revolt.

Active Revolt   Passive revolt does not exhaust the options of the potential rebel. There is always the alternative of active revolt involving activities that advance beyond refusal to cooperate and take the offensive against political communities. The active rebel strikes against the facilities and institutions of the evil state and frontally assaults the castle of its sovereignty. The active rebel is a revolutionary. He uses any tactics that enable him to destroy an unjust political community and erect a better one in its place. His theory of obligation requires him to pursue virtue at all costs and to be intolerant of any evil state irrespective of immediate evils he might commit in the service of ultimate virtue.

The aim of the revolutionary is change—to change the very core of the institutions and basic relationships of his society. While he should not pursue violence for its own sake, he will not let the commission of it deter him from his tasks. He should not act alone as an individual terrorist because that would reduce his effectiveness, render his revolt impotent, and allow tyranny another victory. The tactics he uses are essentially collective as well as overtly activistic.

The revolutionary's sweeping and total confidence in his values is responsible for his use of unlimited force in his quest for justice. This lack of a healthy skepticism and the failure to consider that he may be wrong about even his most treasured ideals may lead him to impatience and potential moral insensitivity. If

---

[15]See Georges Sorel, *Reflections on Violence* (New York: Collier, 1950), for the idea of a general strike. Sorel, however, was an active and not a passive revolutionary.

he feels that justice is unequivocably on his side, he also feels that his actions are the instruments of justice itself and that moral decisions have already been made. To this type of revolutionary, the justice of the future order is so clear and the evil of the present one is so demonstrable that there may be no limits placed on revolutionary action. He recognizes that ineffective or slow action perpetuates tyranny.

For example, there is the case of Marxist-Leninists who overthrew the government of Russia in 1917. Using the political theory of Karl Marx and Friedrich Engels as a basis, Lenin and his fellow Bolsheviks felt that history was an absolute moral guide. The doctrine of dialectical materialism placed justice in the corner of any who would overthrow the capitalist class and who would place workers in power as a step toward the classless society.[16] Buoyed by these absolutes, they saw no contradiction in opposing whole classes of people or in perpetrating acts of terrorism rivaling those of the Czars. Similarly, the cries of "Liberty! Equality! Community!" uttered by revolutionaries of eighteenth-century France led to a reign of terror that saw the guillotining of thousands of real or imagined enemies of the revolution. Nothing and nobody could be allowed to stand in the way of a revolution when justification was absolute and self evident. The only moral consideration was whether the revolution succeeded or failed.

There is no simple moral judgment that can be made about total revolution. It is a very powerful tool that has deep moral implications. For the citizen who finds his political community to be beyond redemption and who has a clear and compelling view of a future order of justice, revolution is a path that cannot be rejected out of hand from either practical or moral considerations. It requires a clear sense of solidarity with fellow victims of tyranny and it is the most effective means available to depose unauthoritative polities. Those who seek a common justice together because they are collective victims of injustice know full well that their obligations as political beings are to each other and to the values that they share and not to any particular regime. And, to use less than maximum efforts in opposing injustice allows tyranny a needless advantage.

Nevertheless, the morality of such total revolutionaries as Lenin or Robespierre is more ambiguous than it might seem to be at first. They were not guilty of omission, to be sure, but the excesses of terror which they permitted tarnishes their revolutionary virtue.

Rebellion   There is another concept of revolt, which we call rebellion instead of revolution. The twentieth-century political thinker Albert Camus best developed this idea in his work, *The Rebel.*[17] Camus argues that given man's history, total revolution leads inevitably to moral excesses. It is wrong because it

---

[16]See George Lichtheim, *Marxism,* Second Edition (New York: F.A. Praeger, 1965) for a complete discussion of these doctrines.
17Albert Camus, *The Rebel* (New York: Vintage Books, 1956).

sanctions unleashing a potentially cataclysmic process that might turn on its initiators—an unlimited attack on all institutions and patterns of society easily threatening the very values that it was meant to affirm. Camus wanted to justify revolt, not nihilism. Camus' rebel must be careful that he does not sacrifice any present person(s) for the sake of a promised future if his rebellion is to be authentically rooted in humanistic values. Justice, a concrete entity, must never be allowed to become a dim abstraction that can serve to approve injustice.

Camus formulated this position on revolt through an analysis of historical theories of rebellion. In pointing out the dangers of these theories he modified them so that their humanitarianism could be preserved and their dangers prevented. "Metaphysical rebellion" is the name that Camus put on one prominent concept of revolution against injustice, referring to it as ". . . the movement by which man protests against his condition and against the whole of creation."[18] Camus felt that metaphysical rebels had the right impulse but went too far. Thinkers like Nietzsche confronted the human condition and concluded that the cause of all the misery in the world was the omniscient and omnipotent God of the Judeo-Christian tradition that, under the guise of "good," permitted men to be tortured and killed. Thus, the metaphysical rebel denounced and attacked this God as the source of all evil. In the place of this God, the deity of absolute justice was raised. One deity was simply replaced by another, equally absolute, equally as prone to unleashing chaos.

This tendency toward excess that Camus sees in metaphysical rebellion can also be seen in what he labeled historical rebellion. In Chapter 3 of *The Rebel*, he traced the transformation of metaphysical rebellion into a theory that is consistent with the "modern" paradigms of agnosticism or atheism that dominated nineteenth- and twentieth-century Western philosophical thought—the efforts of the Marxists to embrace the aims and techniques of metaphysical rebellion without accepting its assumptions. In rejecting deities, they substituted a concept of "history" or "inevitable material forces" that served the same purpose in explaining and justifying and predicting the inevitability of the march of destiny in a grand cataclysm of revolution that would permanently install the "justice" of history fulfilled.

Camus' argument is that no theory of revolution by itself, no matter how it might aim to improve our political communities, is ever morally sufficient as a prescription. It is too easy to forget the ultimate purpose of revolt and to fall into a self-defeating whirlpool of senseless actions without value to guide them unless there is some component in the theory to prevent it. Metaphysical and historical rebellion are not justified by basic values that are clear enough to prevent their misapplication. This is a consequence of assuming values that contain sweeping claims that are asserted instead of morally substantiated.

---

[18]Ibid., p. 23.

Camus did not suggest that revolutions justified in this way would automatically result in nihilism, but he argued that they are vulnerable to such a fate and that the risk is never worth taking. Thus, he rejected both theories by extensively modifying them to retain their moral direction while erecting bulwarks against their dangers. In short, by following the normative method in his thoughts about authority and revolt he avoided the dangers of revolutionary theory while keeping its advantages.

To establish his own alternative to revolt, Camus had only to avoid the excesses of the theories he had criticized by placing within his own theory a doctrine of limits.

In *The Rebel,* Camus puts it this way:

> Does the end justify the means? That is possible. But what will justify the end? To that question, which historical thought leaves pending, rebellion replies: The means.[19]

This direct confrontation of values and techniques of rebellion illustrates that no means that will assault the basic political value of life can be permitted. Events may force such actions, but moral political theory can never endorse them.

This is the context of Camus' crucial distinction between rebellion and revolution. Revolution is a total attempt to replace whole political systems. It has a strong ideology designed to usher in a completely new order to replace an unsalvageable old order. With this aim, it cannot afford to adopt any limits. It must forge a new moral order.

Rebellion is concerned with the ethical implications of living, not merely the abstraction of life. The rebel has few illusions about the future, at least in the world he knows. His healthy skepticism about ultimate truths and about his omniscience helps him to maintain an outlook of humility. He is not sure enough of the absolute validity of his values and his judgment to demand that others die for them. Recognition of error cannot turn back something so permanent as death, and it cannot make amends for immorality. The rebel cannot put aside his vision of justice while he pursues a future millenium. Because his goals seek to advance the social act of living in an imperfect world, he cannot emulate the revolutionary by using techniques that negate life in the present in the name of some future living. Therefore, his values must make a doctrine of limits an integral part of his theory of rebellion.

The rebel must reject any means which devalue those lives he is affirming. When Camus proclaims in Chapter 5 of *The Rebel,*

> Moderation, born of rebellion, can only live by rebellion. It is a perpetual conflict continually created and mastered by intelligence.[20]

[19]Ibid., p. 238.
[20]Ibid.

he means that rebellion is something positive that is limited by equally positive considerations. The rebel who is guided by the intellect uses his intelligence and his political vision in order to strive to protect people and affirm their worth. The limits imposed are not abstract "thou shalt nots." To the contrary, they are logical derivations from previous values. As one defines life in concrete terms, it becomes clear that it is the value of living, of life itself, that limits those who live it even as it supplies them with the drive for their own liberation. This means that values must never be compromised or postponed even by something as drastic and necessary as rebellion. The rebel rejects injustice not for its own sake, but "because it perpetuates the silent hostility that separates the oppressor from the oppressed."[21] He rejects it because it slays the communion and political solidarity of living. Ruled out, therefore, are such things as deceit, perpetuation of servitude, and mindless violence. All are proscribed because "life in the community is the supreme value for the rebel,"[22] and these actions are antipolitical—they seek to divide instead of to integrate.

The position of rebellion is a formidable one. In its pursuit of moral consistency it substitutes the citizen's considered basic political value for the revolutionary's metaphysical and illusive "lesson of history"—a penultimate for an ultimate. To be sure, it is not the easiest course for the victim of tyranny. It puts a premium on values instead of vendetta. It must be planned and executed with a great deal of both ethical sensitivity and careful strategy. Although it is not easier than revolution, rebellion is better because it serves humanistic political values consistently while revolutionary zeal does not. Rebellion neither commits the sin of omission (it does oppose tyranny with vigor) nor does it commit the revolutionary sin of commission—of using tactics that are inconsistent with what authority and revolt are all about. In effect, it is not a theory of revolt itself but an improvement on the theory of revolution that came from a critical moral analysis of the political theory of revolution. If examples of rebellion are hard to find in history, it is not so much because it is impossible but because too many people choose not to think when it really counts. The Gandhis and the Camuses of the world prove it can be done.

PRESCRIPTION AND PERSPECTIVES

The most important principle to keep in mind is what is most appropriately termed "community mindedness." Human beings who share the same territory depend on just political interaction for decent lives. Without a way to relate justly to others, to realize the advantages and blunt the dangers of human

[21]Fred Wilhoite, *Beyond Nihilism* (Baton Rouge: Louisiana State University Press, 1968), pp. 82–83.
[22]Camus, op. cit., pp. 285–286.

interdependence, the citizen is lost. At best, his political life will come close to the depressing picture sketched by Hobbes in his *Leviathan* when he described political life without a just order as "Poor, nasty, brutish and short." Luckily, Hobbes' pictures need not be an accurate one. Authoritative political communities are within our reach if each citizen undertakes the obligations that provide the political life of a good community and make possible a just environment for all citizens. In other words, values and obligations that recognize the individuality of each human being and allow that individuality to flourish equally are what is necessary. They will allow each person to be secure in his public dealings with others. Only in such an environment can one pursue his individual needs and interests without the threats or exploitation that can only lead to stifling conformity, regimentation, or worse. If political relationships can be kept on a plane that will prevent inequality and will recognize that our individuality is partly the result of our relationships with others then we can bring the ideal of political authority to reality. And we can thereby deny the dark potentiality in Hobbes' warnings.

The citizen with such attitudes on authority and revolt is community minded because he has the need for a just politics for all uppermost in mind. In this sense, community mindedness and individualism are complementary values in obligation. Such a community orientation that does not forget individual needs will lead to theories on authority and revolt that make individual dignity possible because it is nothing more than the commitment to the search for social justice. The requirement is that we must keep the values and theories of such an authoritative community prominent in our decisions on whether to revolt against or obey a given political community.

The importance of this principle lies in its applicability to the many theories of revolt and authority worthy of consideration. The best approach is to view the various alternatives as being on a continuum that has a definite starting point, a specific end and contains guides for applying appropriate courses of action to events. After all, the major problem associated with the whole concept of revolt is how to stop the denial of justice in political communities. If our polities are immoral we must remember that our obligations are to each other and not to specific institutions and that our common ideal of authority compels us to seek it if we do not have it. Justice is our goal and we have only to apply it consistently: in means as well as in ends in spite of the difficulty of pursuing rational courses in turbulent times. Our general principle of tactics must come from the same roots as our theories of obligation. What we must do is clear enough. We must try the least coercive means first and escalate only if we fail. This is the only way to limit the force of our revolt. Injustice can only be opposed in the interest of each citizen and we will try not to disrupt his life-style and, more importantly, to preserve his dignity and rights as much as possible. Human beings are too valuable to be sacrificed.

Thus, the first step must always be at least a fair consideration of provisional obligation. One should weigh the advantages as well as the disadvantages of his political community very carefully before making a decision on revolt. There are such things as honest mistakes or temporary lapses of judgment that have bad consequences only in the short run and can often be corrected swiftly if complaints are effectively articulated by citizens. There is no pressing need for revolt against such government failures, since they do not prove the state to be utterly corrupt. In other words, every temporarily unjust institution or distasteful policy is not grounds for withdrawal of political obligation. There should be clear and continuing violation of basic political values before one declares irrevocable opposition to some of one's fellow citizens and the community they share with us. Continued obligation, of course, does not mean that acquiescence in all aspects of the state is necessary. One may still work to change what is wrong even in the short run.

If provisional obligation cannot be justified, we can always just ignore our problems, although that would merely perpetuate them. Our best counsel is to try and do something if the situation warrants it. It is both good morality and wise self-interest. The next step on the continuum should fall short of total opposition. Civil disobedience is frequently sufficient to get recalcitrant polities back on the right track. The shock of citizens taking great personal risks without personal benefit other than the hope of justice is often enough to jar even violently unjust states to their senses and to cause effective change. While its effect was not felt swiftly enough to suit many, the antiwar movement in the United States in the 1960s and 1970s was one reason which caused the American government to withdraw our military forces from Vietnam and to undertake a continuing review of the whole purposes and designs of the national foreign policy. While full-scale revolution might have accomplished the same thing, it would have been a tragic case of "overkill" in revolt. What is more, such an action would run an unnecessary risk of promoting a worse regime once the Pandora's box of total opposition was opened. Thus, the citizen who has a genuine concern for political relationships and stable and just interactions with other citizens should not leap too far too fast—civil disobedience is a logical next step. If he cannot or does not want to do that, he should carefully monitor the serious acts of civil disobedience of others to see if they have the desired effect. As long as there are many good aspects of a political community and as long as civil disobedience has at least an outside chance to reestablish authority, it is the most logical extension of sincere obligations and desire for justice.

If civil disobedience is insufficient to redeem a polity gone awry (and a polity's reaction toward legitimate civil disobedience is one good index thereof), passive resistance is the next logical step. It is morally preferable to potentially more violent forms of revolt because the passive resistor refrains from committing overt acts of violence against others. This is balanced by the fact that the mere existence of any situation of total opposition, passive or not, is likely to produce massive social displacement for citizens, not to mention its encouragement of violent acts of reprisal by the state in its attempt to defend itself. For the pacifist whose doctrine of limits absolutely prohibits any compromise with violence, this is the most radical step he can take. Even for nonpacifists who nevertheless try to avoid violence, this is a good step to follow after civil disobedience fails. We have to have some faith that it might be just effective enough to overthrow tyranny and reestablish an authoritative polity. If we are fortunate enough to have our faith justified, more violent forms of revolt are surely "overkill" and should not be risked until we know they cannot be avoided. Thus, it is morally safer to try passive resistance before active resistance in the hope of minimizing coercion. Even if coercion can never be totally avoided, we must still try to hold it at arm's length as long as possible.

The final point on the continuum can either be revolution or rebellion, accepting Camus' distinction between full revolt without or with a doctrine of limits. Unless the revolutionary can be sure his cause is absolutely correct and unless he does not place a high value on the life and rights of all citizens, all-out revolution should be rejected. Its cost is too high for its value. Camus is quite correct when he says that it is immoral to buy justice with the coin of injustice. Sound political values cannot be laid aside for the duration of the revolution so that we might destroy those whom we hate in order to hasten the day of justice. It is a moral contradiction to do so. To avoid the moral defects inherent in revolution the citizen who must overthrow a political community without merit must be meritorious himself in his ideas and deeds. His values can never be shunted aside if he really respects them. Rebellion is preferable because it unites the diminution of coercion with the advantages of humanism. The rebel need not hang his head after the battle and wonder whether his accomplishments were worth their cost. He knows that he always acted in a way that reflected justice in ends as well as means.

In the final analysis, the citizen who judges his political community to be wanting in authority knows that his values and loyalties to fellow citizens require him to avoid unnecessary violence. He should cast about for tactics that enable him to eradicate injustice with only as much violence as is necessary to accomplish his aims and stay within moral bounds. Thus, if a less vehement step than rebellion works, that is ideal.

Social or political change is a cataclysmic process that cannot be accomplished without great coercion, whether directly violent or more subtle but not less insidious. We must not minimize the effect on people's fortunes, safety, and even sanity that such change brings. Nevertheless, if the rebel has tried to find less coercive ways to reestablish an authoritative political community and he has failed, then he must push. Tyranny, too, has its costs. The rebel can be secure in the knowledge that he recognized and met his obligations and that he brought morality to immoral times. As long as he acts in a morally serious fashion and keeps his doctrine of limits with him, the rebel's acts will always be an affirmation of justice and a denial of injustice.

In the end, what is required is judgment. The citizen must know what he values and why and how to derive a theory of political obligation from that. If he has done so and must face tyranny, he will be in a position to sidestep the dim alternatives of unknowing acquiesence in injustice or immoral, blind, and undirected opposition to everything. He can judge carefully even in an hour of desperation. He can make authority meaningful by affirming justice without nihilism.

SUGGESTIONS FOR SUPPLEMENTARY READING

Authority

Berlin, Isaiah, *Four Essays on Liberty* (London: Oxford University Press, 1969).

Cassirer, Ernst, *The Myth of the State* (New Haven: Yale University Press, 1946).

Dahl, Robert, *After the Revolution: Authority in the Good Society* (New Haven: Yale University Press, 1970).

Hobbes, Thomas, *Leviathan,* many publications.

_____ , *De Cive,* many publications.

Machiavelli, Niccolo, *The Prince,* many publications.

_____ , *The Discourses,* many publications.

Plato, *The Republic,* many publications.

Rousseau, Jean Jacques, *The Social Contract,* many publications.

Thoreau, *Slavery in Massachusetts,* many publications.

Walzer, Michael, *Obligations,* (Cambridge, Mass.: Harvard University Press, 1970).

Revolt

Berman, Marshall, *The Politics of Authenticity,* (New York: Atheneum, 1970).

Burke, Edmund, *Reflections on the Revolution in France* (Garden City: Dolphin, 1961).

Camus, Albert, *The Rebel* (New York: Vintage Books, 1956).

_____ , *Resistance, Rebellion and Death* (New York: Alfred A. Knopf, 1960).

Hanson, D. and R.B. Fowler, *Obligation and Dissent* (Boston: Little, Brown and Company, 1971).

Paine, Thomas, *The Rights of Man* (Garden City: Dolphin, 1961).

_____ , *Common Sense,* many publications.

Sorel, Georges, *Reflections on Violence* (New York: Collier, 1950).

Spitz, David, Editor, *Political Theory and Social Change* (New York: Atherton, 1967).

Thoreau, Henry, *Civil Disobedience,* many publications.

Index

167